PRACTICE – ASSESS – DIAGNOSE

180 Days of SOCIAL STUDIES
for Kindergarten

W9-BDC-518

Author
Kathy Flynn, M.Ed.

SHELL EDUCATION

Publishing Credits

Corinne Burton, M.A.Ed., *Publisher*
Conni Medina, M.A.Ed., *Managing Editor*
Emily R. Smith, M.A.Ed., *Content Director*
Veronique Bos, *Creative Director*

**Developed and Produced by
Focus Strategic Communications, Inc.**

Project Manager: Adrianna Edwards
Editor: Cathy Fraccaro
Designer and Compositor: Ruth Dwight
Proofreader: Francine Geraci
Photo Researcher: Paula Joiner
Art: Deborah Crowle

Image Credits

Standards

© 2014 Mid-continent Research for Education and Learning (McREL)
© 2010 National Council for the Social Studies (NCSS), The College, Career, and Civic Life (C3) Framework for Social Studies State Standards: Guidance for Enhancing the Rigor of K–12 Civics, Economics, Geography, and History

> For information on how this resource meets national and other state standards, see pages 12–14. You may also review this information by visiting our website at www.teachercreatedmaterials.com/administrators/correlations/ and following the on-screen directions.

Shell Education

A division of Teacher Created Materials
5301 Oceanus Drive
Huntington Beach, CA 92649-1030
www.tcmpub.com/shell-education

ISBN 978-1-4258-1392-5
©2018 Shell Educational Publishing, Inc.

Table of Contents

Introduction

In the complex global world of the 21st century, it is essential for citizens to have the foundational knowledge and analytic skills to understand the barrage of information surrounding them. An effective social studies program will provide students with these analytic skills and prepare them to understand and make intentional decisions about their country and the world. A well-designed social studies program develops active citizens who are able to consider multiple viewpoints and the possible consequences of various decisions.

The four disciplines of social studies enable students to understand their relationships with other people—those who are similar and those from diverse backgrounds. Students come to appreciate the foundations of the American democratic system and the importance of civic involvement. They have opportunities to understand the historic and economic forces that have resulted in the world and United States of today. They will also explore geography to better understand the nature of Earth and the effects of human interactions.

It is essential that social studies addresses more than basic knowledge. In each grade, content knowledge is a vehicle for students to engage in deep, rich thinking. They must problem solve, make decisions, work cooperatively as well as alone, make connections, and make reasoned value judgments. The world and the United States are rapidly changing. Students must be prepared for the world they will soon lead.

The Need for Practice

To be successful in today's social studies classrooms, students must understand both basic knowledge and the application of ideas to new or novel situations. They must be able to discuss and apply their ideas in coherent and rational ways. Practice is essential if they are to internalize social studies concepts, skills, and big ideas. Practice is crucial to help students have the experience and confidence to apply the critical-thinking skills needed to be active citizens in a global society.

Introduction (cont.)

Understanding Assessment

In addition to providing opportunities for frequent practice, teachers must be able to assess students' understanding of social studies concepts, big ideas, vocabulary, and reasoning. This is important so teachers can effectively address students' misconceptions and gaps, build on their current understanding, and challenge their thinking at an appropriate level. Assessment is a long-term process that involves careful analysis of student responses from a multitude of sources. In the social studies context, this could include classroom discussions, projects, presentations, practice sheets, or tests. When analyzing the data, it is important for teachers to reflect on how their teaching practices may have influenced students' responses and to identify those areas where additional instruction may be required. Essentially, the data gathered from assessment should be used to inform instruction: to slow down, to continue as planned, to speed up, or to reteach in a new way.

Best Practices for This Series

- Use the practice pages to introduce important social studies topics to your students.

- Use the Weekly Topics and Themes chart from pages 5–7 to align the content to what you're covering in class. Then, treat the pages in this book as jumping off points for that content.

- Use the practice pages as formative assessment of the key social studies disciplines: history, civics, geography, and economics.

- Use the weekly themes to engage students in content that is new to them.

- Encourage students to independently learn more about the topics introduced in this series.

- Challenge students with some of the more complex weeks by leading teacher-directed discussions of the vocabulary and concepts presented.

- Support students in practicing the varied types of questions asked throughout the practice pages.

- Use the texts in this book to extend your teaching of close reading, responding to text-dependent questions, and providing evidence for answers.

How to Use This Book

180 Days of Social Studies offers teachers and parents a full page of social studies practice for each day of the school year.

Weekly Structure

These activities reinforce grade-level skills across a variety of social studies concepts. The content and questions are provided as full practice pages, making them easy to prepare and implement as part of a classroom routine or for homework.

Every practice page provides content, questions, and/or tasks that are tied to a social studies topic and standard. Students are given opportunities for regular practice in social studies, allowing them to build confidence through these quick standards-based activities.

Weekly Topics and Themes

The activities are organized by a weekly topic within one of the four social studies disciplines: history, civics, geography, and economics. The following chart shows the topics that are covered during each week of instruction:

Week	Discipline	Social Studies Topic	NCSS Theme
1	History	Chronological sequencing	Time, continuity, and change
2	Civics	Rules at school	Civic ideals and practices; Power, authority, and governance
3	Geography	Location and relative position	People, places, and environments
4	Economics	Understanding basic needs	Production, distribution, and consumption
5	History	National holidays—Remembering the past	Culture
6	Civics	Rules at home	Civic ideals and practices; Power, authority, and governance
7	Geography	Location and relative position	People, places, and environments
8	Economics	Where we get food	Production, distribution, and consumption
9	History	National holidays—Saying thank you	Culture
10	Civics	Why we have rules	Civic ideals and practices; Power, authority, and governance

How to Use This Book (cont.)

Week	Discipline	Social Studies Topic	NCSS Theme
11	Geography	Maps—Classroom	People, places, and environments
12	Economics	Understanding wants	Production, distribution, and consumption
13	History	American symbols	Culture; Time, continuity, and change
14	Civics	Being a good citizen—Cooperation and sharing	Civic ideals and practices; Individual development and identity
15	Geography	Maps—School	People, places, and environments
16	Economics	Community helpers/jobs	Production, distribution, and consumption
17	History	American symbols	Culture; Time, continuity, and change
18	Civics	Being a good citizen—Respect for things around us	Civic ideals and practices; Individual development and identity
19	Geography	Landforms and bodies of water	People, places, and environments
20	Economics	Community helpers/jobs	Production, distribution, and consumption
21	History	Famous Americans	People, places, and environments
22	Civics	Being a good citizen in the United States	Civic ideals and practices; Power, authority, and governance
23	Geography	Changing seasons—Geographic regions	People, places, and environments
24	Economics	How we can get things we need/want	Production, distribution, and consumption
25	History	Famous Americans	People, places, and environments
26	Civics	Conflict resolution—Listening and respecting	Civic ideals and practices; Individual development and identity

How to Use This Book (cont.)

Week	Discipline	Social Studies Topic	NCSS Theme
27	Geography	Out in the weather—Clothes and activities for the weather	People, places, and environments
28	Economics	Choice and scarcity	Production, distribution, and consumption
29	History	Life today and long ago	Time, continuity, and change
30	Civics	Conflict resolution—Voting and decision making in the classroom	Civic ideals and practices; Power, authority and governance
31	Geography	Our school community	People, places, and environments
32	Economics	What is money?	Production, distribution, and consumption
33	History	Jobs long ago and today	Time, continuity, and change
34	Civics	Being a good citizen in the United States	Civic ideals and practices; Power, authority, and governance
35	Geography	My neighborhood	People, places, and environments
36	Economics	American coins	Production, distribution, and consumption

How to Use This Book *(cont.)*

Using the Practice Pages

Practice pages provide instruction and assessment opportunities for each day of the school year. Days 1 to 4 provide content in short texts or graphics followed by related questions or tasks. Day 5 provides an application task based on the week's work.

All four social studies disciplines are practiced. There are nine weeks of topics for each discipline. The discipline is indicated on the margin of each page.

Day 1: Students read a text about the weekly topic and answer questions. This day provides a general introduction to the week's topic.

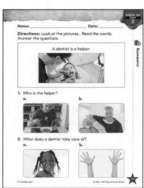

Day 2: Students read a text and answer questions. Typically, this content is more specialized than Day 1.

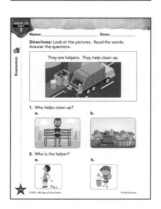

Day 3: Students analyze a primary source or other graphic (chart, table, graph, or infographic) related to the weekly topic and answer questions.

How to Use This Book (cont.)

Using the Practice Pages (cont.)

Day 4: Students analyze an image or text and answer questions. Then, students make connections to their own lives.

Day 5: Students analyze a primary source or other graphic and respond to it using knowledge they've gained throughout the week. This day serves as an application of what they've learned.

Diagnostic Assessment

Teachers can use the practice pages as diagnostic assessments. The data analysis tools included with the book enable teachers or parents to quickly score students' work and monitor their progress. Teachers and parents can see which skills students may need to target further to develop proficiency.

Students will learn skills to support informational text analysis, primary source analysis, how to make connections to self, and how to apply what they learned. To assess students' learning in these areas, check their answers based on the answer key or use the *Response Rubric* (page 200) for constructed-response questions that you want to evaluate more deeply. Then, record student scores on the *Practice Page Item Analysis* (page 204). You may also wish to complete a *Student Item Analysis by Discipline* for each student (pages 206–207). These charts are also provided in the Digital Resources as PDFs, *Microsoft Word*® files, and *Microsoft Excel*® files. Teachers can input data into the electronic files directly on the computer, or they can print the pages. See page 208 for more information.

Diagnostic Assessment *(cont.)*

Practice Page Item Analyses

Every four weeks, follow these steps:

- Choose the four-week range you're assessing in the first row.

- Write or type the students' names in the far left column. Depending on the number of students, more than one copy of the form may be needed.

  - The skills are indicated across the top of the chart.

- For each student, record how many correct answers they gave and/or their rubric scores in the appropriate columns. There will be four numbers in each cell, one for each week. You can view which students are or are not understanding the social studies concepts or student progress after multiple opportunities to respond to specific text types or question forms.

- Review students' work for the first four sections. Add the scores for each student, and write that sum in the far right column. Use these scores as benchmarks to determine how each student is performing.

Student Item Analyses by Discipline

For each discipline, follow these steps:

- Write or type the student's name on the top of the charts.

  - The skills are indicated across the tops of the charts.

- Select the appropriate discipline and week.

- For each student, record how many correct answers they gave and/or their rubric scores in the appropriate columns. You can view which students are or are not understanding each social studies discipline or student progress after multiple opportunities to respond to specific text types or question forms.

How to Use This Book *(cont.)*

Using the Results to Differentiate Instruction

Once results are gathered and analyzed, teachers can use the results to inform the way they differentiate instruction. The data can help determine which social studies skills and content are the most difficult for students and which students need additional instructional support and continued practice. Depending on how often the practice pages are scored, results can be considered for instructional support on a weekly or monthly basis.

Whole-Class Support

The results of the diagnostic analysis may show that the entire class is struggling with a particular concept or group of concepts. If these concepts have been taught in the past, this indicates that further instruction or reteaching is necessary. If these concepts have not been taught in the past, this data is a great preassessment and demonstrate that students do not have a working knowledge of the concepts. Thus, careful planning for the length of the unit(s) or lesson(s) must be considered, and extra front-loading may be required.

Small-Group or Individual Support

The results of the diagnostic analysis may show that an individual or a small group of students is struggling with a particular concept or group of concepts. If these concepts have been taught in the past, this indicates that further instruction or reteaching is necessary. Consider pulling aside these students while others are working independently to instruct further on the concept(s). You can also use the result to help identify individuals or groups of proficient students who are ready for enrichment or above-grade-level instruction. These students may benefit from independent learning contracts or more challenging activities.

Digital Resources

The Digital Resources contain PDFs and editable digital copies of the rubrics and item analysis pages. See page 208 for more information.

Standards Correlations

Shell Education is committed to producing educational materials that are research and standards based. In this effort, we have correlated all products to the academic standards of all 50 states, the District of Columbia, the Department of Defense Dependent Schools, and the Canadian provinces.

How to Find Standards Correlations

To print a customized correlation report of this product for your state, visit our website at **www.teachercreatedmaterials.com/administrators/correlations/** and follow the online directions. If you require assistance in printing correlation reports, please contact the Customer Service Department at 1-877-777-3450.

Purpose and Intent of Standards

The Every Student Succeeds Act (ESSA) mandates that all states adopt challenging academic standards that help students meet the goal of college and career readiness. While many states already adopted academic standards prior to ESSA, the act continues to hold states accountable for detailed and comprehensive standards.

Standards are designed to focus instruction and guide adoption of curricula. Standards are statements that describe the criteria necessary for students to meet specific academic goals. They define the knowledge, skills, and content students should acquire at each level. Standards are also used to develop standardized tests to evaluate students' academic progress. Teachers are required to demonstrate how their lessons meet state standards. State standards are used in the development of all of our products, so educators can be assured they meet the academic requirements of each state.

NCSS Standards and the C3 Framework

The lessons in this book are aligned to the National Council for the Social Studies (NCSS) standards and the C3 Framework. The chart on pages 5–7 lists the NCSS themes used throughout this book.

McREL Compendium

Each year, McREL analyzes state standards and revises the compendium to produce a general compilation of national standards. The chart on pages 13–14 correlates specific McREL standards to the content covered each week.

Standards Correlations *(cont.)*

Week	McREL Standard
1	Understands family life now and in the past, and family life in various places long ago.
2	Understands the sources, purposes, and functions of law, and the importance of the rule of law for the protection of individual rights and the common good.
3	Understands the characteristics and uses of maps, globes, and other geographic tools and technologies.
4	Understands basic features of market structures and exchanges.
5	Understands how democratic values came to be, and how they have been exemplified by people, events, and symbols.
6	Understands ideas about civic life, politics, and government.
7	Knows the location of places, geographic features, and patterns of the environment.
8	Understands basic features of market structures and exchanges.
9	Understands how democratic values came to be, and how they have been exemplified by people, events, and symbols.
10	Understands ideas about civic life, politics, and government.
11	Knows the location of places, geographic features, and patterns of the environment.
12	Understands basic features of market structures and exchanges.
13	Understands how democratic values came to be, and how they have been exemplified by people, events, and symbols.
14	Understands the sources, purposes, and functions of law, and the importance of the rule of law for the protection of individual rights and the common good.
15	Understands the physical and human characteristics of place Understands the nature and complexity of Earth's cultural mosaics.
16	Understands the roles government plays in the United States economy.
17	Understands family life now and in the past, and family life in various places long ago.
18	Understands ideas about civic life, politics, and government.
19	Understands the concept of regions Understands the physical and human characteristics of place.
20	Understands that scarcity of productive resources requires choices that generate opportunity costs.
21	Understands the folklore and other cultural contributions from various regions of the United States and how they helped to form a national heritage.
22	Understands ideas about civic life, politics, and government.

Standards Correlations *(cont.)*

Week	McREL Standard
23	Understands the physical and human characteristics of place. Understands the patterns of human settlement and their causes.
24	Understands that scarcity of productive resources requires choices that generate opportunity costs. Understands basic features of market structures and exchanges.
25	Understands the folklore and other cultural contributions from various regions of the United States and how they helped to form a national heritage.
26	Understands ideas about civic life, politics, and government.
27	Understands the physical and human characteristics of place. Understands how human actions modify the physical environment.
28	Understands that scarcity of productive resources requires choices that generate opportunity costs.
29	Understands major discoveries in science and technology, some of their social and economic effects, and the major scientists and inventors responsible for them.
30	Understands how certain character traits enhance citizens' ability to fulfill personal and civic responsibilities. Understands the roles of voluntarism and organized groups in American social and political life.
31	Understands the changes that occur in the meaning, use, distribution and importance of resources. Understands how human actions modify the physical environment.
32	Understands that scarcity of productive resources requires choices that generate opportunity costs.
33	Understands the history of a local community and how communities in North America varied long ago.
34	Understands how certain character traits enhance citizens' ability to fulfill personal and civic responsibilities.
35	Understands the characteristics and uses of spatial organization of Earth's surface. Understands the changes that occur in the meaning, use, distribution and importance of resources.
36	Understands that scarcity of productive resources requires choices that generate opportunity costs.

Name:_____ **Date:**_____

Directions: Look at the pictures. Who is young? Who is old? Draw lines to put the people in order, from the youngest to the oldest.

History

History

Name: _____ **Date:** _____

Directions: Look at the pictures. Read the words. Circle the correct answers.

1. What do you do at school?

a.

b.

2. What do you do at home?

a.

b.

Name:_____ **Date:**_____

Directions: Look at the pictures. Read the words.
Circle the correct answer.

What We Will Do Today

1. What will you do at school today?

a. **b.**

Name:_____ Date:_____

Directions: Look at the pictures. Cut ✂---them out.
Paste GLUE⊳ them on the time line.

History

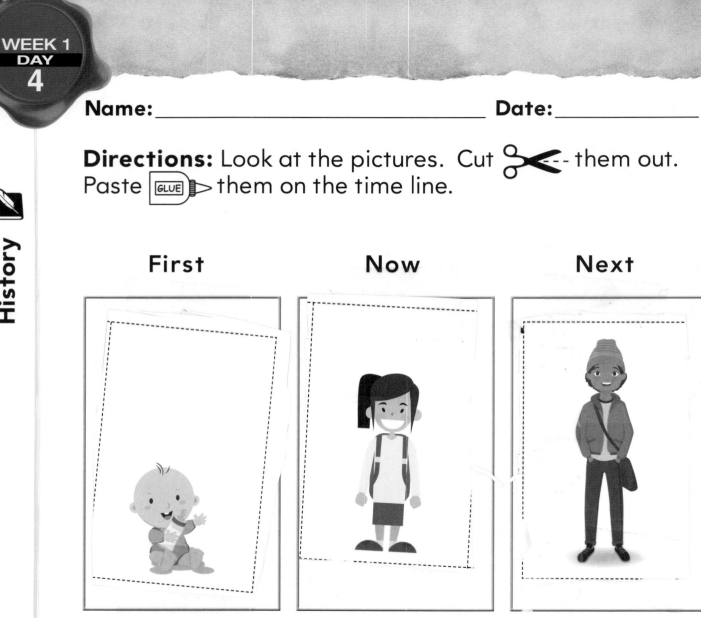

First   Now   Next

Name: _____ **Date:** _____

Directions: Read the story. Then, draw pictures.

> My name is Jamie. I go to school. I help on the farm. When I grow up, I want to work in a store.

Draw Jamie as a grown-up.

Draw yourself as a grown-up.

Civics

Name: _____ **Date:** _____

Directions: Look at the pictures. Read the words. Circle the correct answers.

We have rules at school.

Share.

Clean up.

Keep your hands to yourself.

1. Which picture is a rule?

a.

b.

2. How do rules make us feel?

a.

b.

Name:_____ **Date:**_____

Directions: Look at the pictures. Read the words. Circle the correct answers.

We have rules.

Sit quietly.   Raise hand.   Listen.

1. Which picture is a rule?

a.

b.

2. Which picture is a rule?

a.

b.

Name: _____ **Date:** _____

Civics

Directions: Look at the pictures. Read the words. Circle the correct answer.

Walk.   Stay in line.

1. Which picture is a rule?

   a.   **b.**

2. Draw a rule.

51392—180 Days of Social Studies

Name:_____ **Date:**_____

Directions: Look at the pictures. Read the words.
Draw your rules.

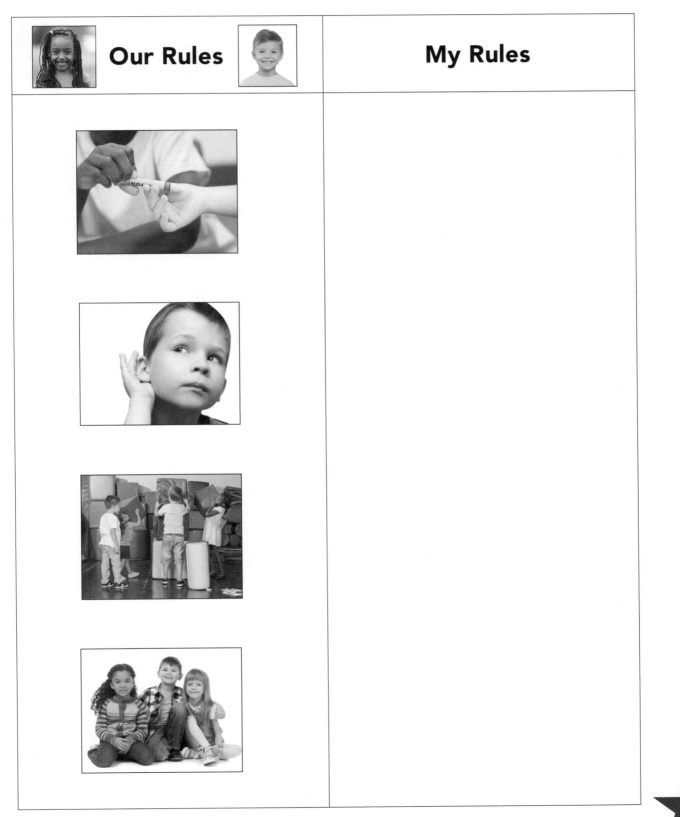

Our Rules	My Rules

51392—180 Days of Social Studies

Civics

Name:_____ **Date:**_____

Directions: Look at the children following rules in the picture.

Draw a picture of children following another rule.

Name: _____ **Date:** _____

Directions: Look at the pictures. Read the words. Circle the correct answers.

over   under

1. The dog is _____ the house.

   a.   **b.**

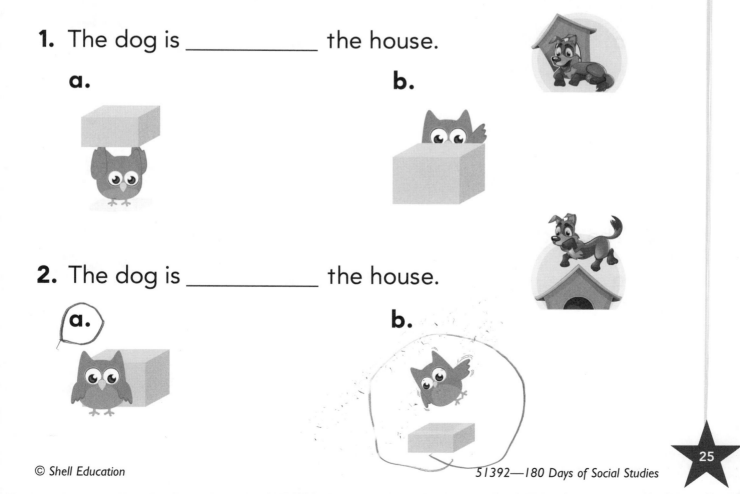

2. The dog is _____ the house.

   a.   **b.**

Name: _____ **Date:** _____

Geography

Directions: Look at the pictures. Read the words. Circle the correct answers.

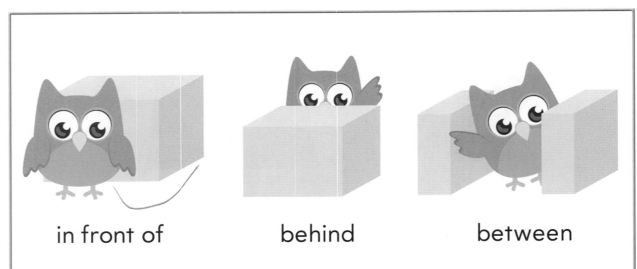

in front of   behind   between

1. The dog is _____ the house.

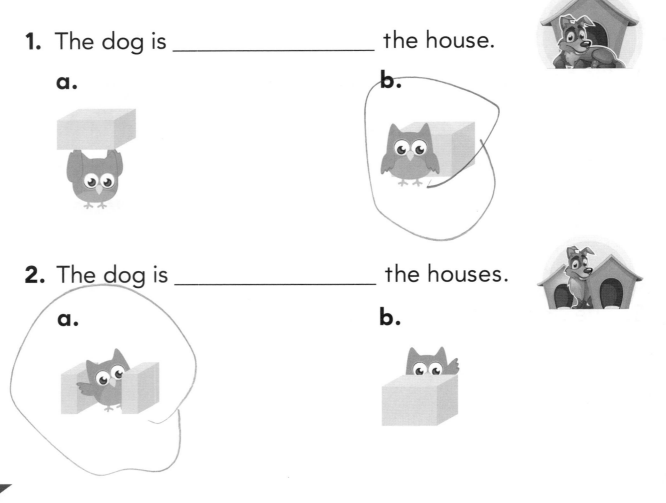

a.

b.

2. The dog is _____ the houses.

a.

b.

51392—180 Days of Social Studies

Name: _____ **Date:** _____

Directions: Look at the pictures. Circle the two pictures that are alike.

Draw a bear under a table.

Geography

Name: _____ **Date:** _____

Directions: Look at the picture. Read the words. Circle the correct answer.

I am between the boxes.

1. Where is the girl?

a.

b.

2. Draw yourself under a box.

51392—180 Days of Social Studies   © *Shell Education*

Name: _____ **Date:** _____

Directions: Look at the pictures. Where are the animals? Match the pictures that are alike.

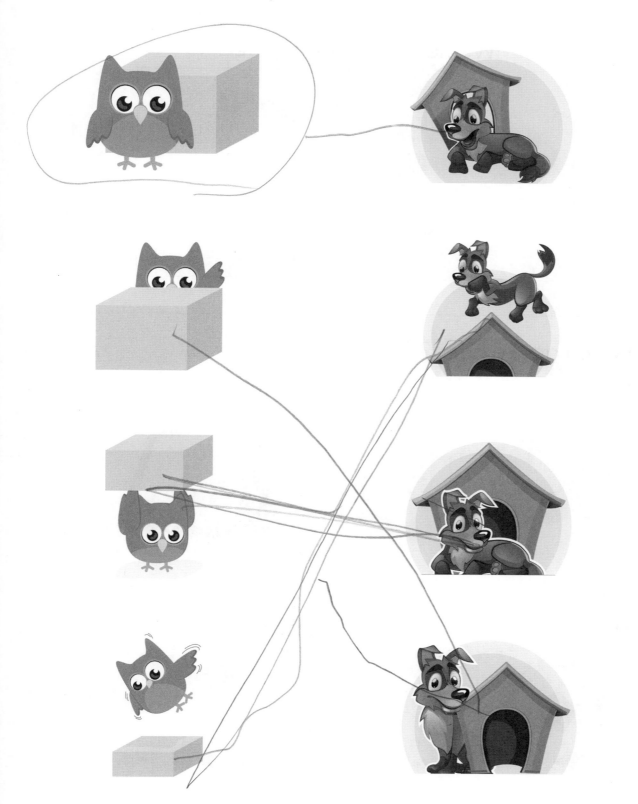

Economics

Name:_____ **Date:**_____

Directions: Look at the pictures. Read the words. Circle the correct answers.

We need food and water.

1. Which do we need?

   a.

   b.

2. Which do we need?

   a.

   b.

   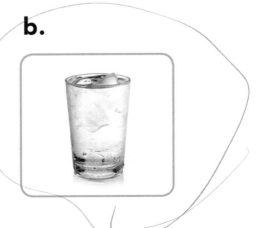

Name:_____ **Date:**_____

Directions: Look at the pictures. Read the words.
Circle the correct answers.

We need a home.

1. Which do we need?

a.

b.

2. Which do we need?

a.

b.

Economics

Name: _____ **Date:** _____

Directions: Look at the pictures. Read the words. Circle the correct answer.

We need clothes.

1. Which do we need?

a.

b.

2. Draw your clothes.

Name:_____ **Date:**_____

Directions: Look at the pictures. Read the words.

We need all these things.

Draw a picture of yourself with things you need.

Economics

Name:_____ Date:_____

Economics

Directions: Look at the pictures. Circle things we need.

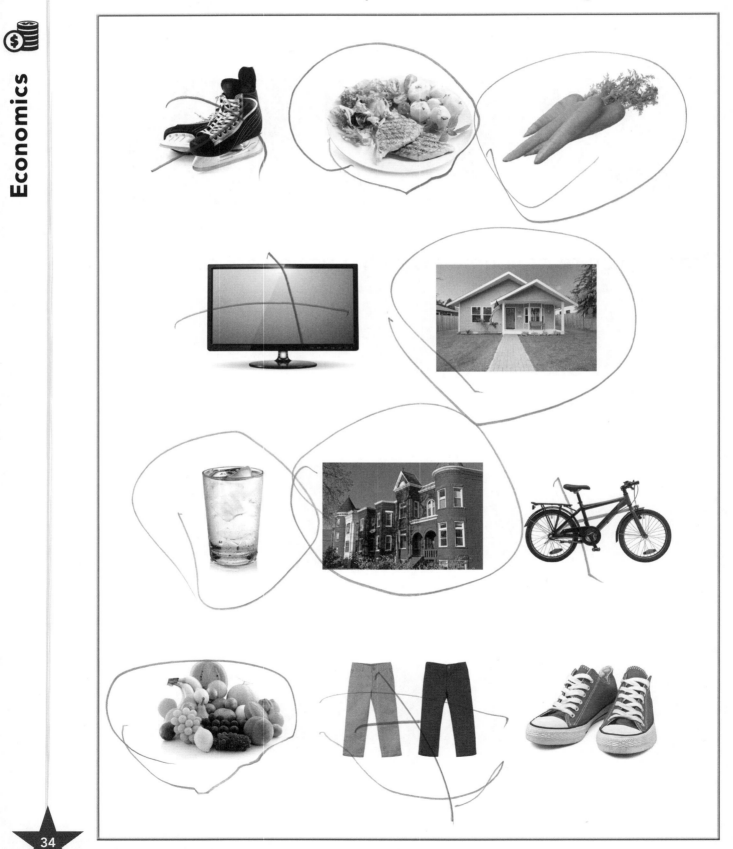

51392—180 Days of Social Studies

Name:_____ Date:_____

Directions: Look at the pictures. Read the words.
Circle the correct answers.

America Celebrates

We have holidays. We have fun with our families.

1. Which picture shows holiday fun?

a.   **b.**

2. Which holiday shows we like our country?

a.   **b.**

History

Name:_____ **Date:**_____

Directions: Look at the picture. Read the words. Circle the correct answers.

July 4 is our country's birthday. We have parades.

1. How do we celebrate on July 4?
   a.   **b.**

2. What else do people do on July 4?
   a.   **b.**

Name: _____ **Date:** _____

Directions: Look at the picture. Read the words. Circle the correct answers.

George Washington

He was a president. He was born in February. Presidents Day is in February.

1. When did Washington live?
a. long ago   **b.** today

2. How did Washington write?

a.   **b.**

History

Name:_____ Date:_____

Directions: Look at the picture. Read the words. Circle the correct answer.

Abraham Lincoln

He lived long ago. His home was a log cabin. He helped people.

1. Where did Lincoln live?

a.

b.

2. Draw yourself in a log cabin.

Name:_____ **Date:**_____

Directions: Look at the pictures.

George Washington's
home

Abraham Lincoln's
home

Draw your home.

Civics

Name:_____ **Date:**_____

Directions: Look at the pictures. Read the words. Circle the correct answers.

We have rules at home.

Share. Clean up. Listen.

1. Which picture is a rule?

a. **b.**

2. Which picture is a rule at home and at school?

a. **b.**

51392—180 Days of Social Studies

Name:_____ **Date:**_____

Directions: Look at the pictures. Read the words.
Circle the correct answers.

We have mealtime rules.

Set the table.   Clear the dishes.   Eat nicely.

1. Which picture is a rule?

a.

b.

2. Which rule helps at home?

a.

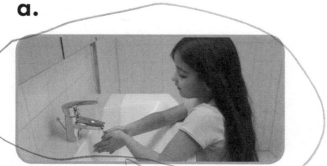

b.

Civics

Name: _____ **Date:** _____

Directions: Look at the pictures. Read the words. Circle the correct answer.

We have bedtime rules.

Brush your teeth.   Go to bed.   Go to sleep.

1. Which picture is a bedtime rule?

a.

b.

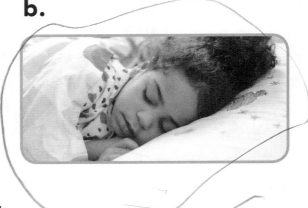

2. Draw yourself going to bed.

Name: _____ **Date:** _____

Directions: Look at the pictures. Draw your rules.

Our Rules	My Rules

Civics

Civics

Name:_____ **Date:**_____

Directions: Look at the pictures. Circle the children who are following rules.

Draw two rules in your home.

Name:_____ Date:_____

Directions: Look at the pictures. Read the words.
Circle the correct answers.

in

on

1. The dog is _____ the house.

a.

b.

2. The dog is _____ the house.

a.

b.

Geography

Name: _____ **Date:** _____

Directions: Look at the pictures. Read the words.
Circle the correct answers.

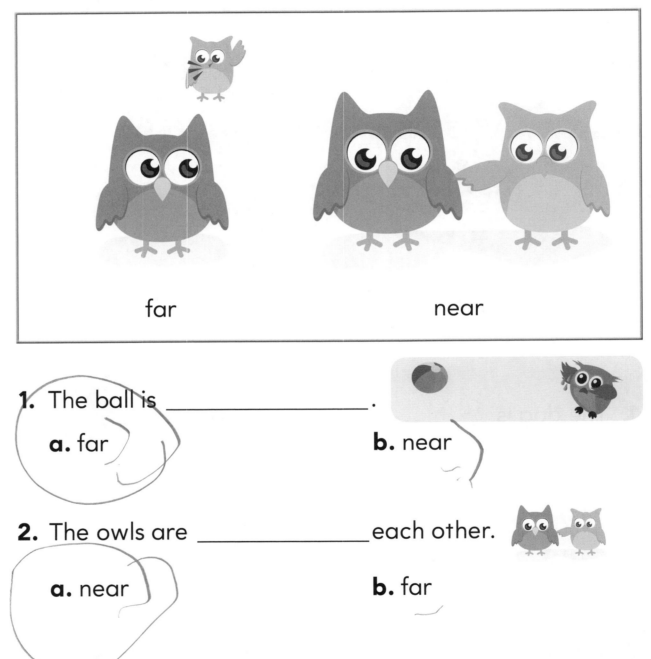

far   near

1. The ball is _____.

   a. far   **b.** near

2. The owls are _____ each other.

   a. near   **b.** far

51392—180 Days of Social Studies

Name:_____ **Date:**_____

Directions: Look at the pictures. Circle the ones that are alike.

Draw a bear in bed.

Geography

Geography

Name: _____ **Date:** _____

Directions: Look at the pictures and words. Draw a picture.

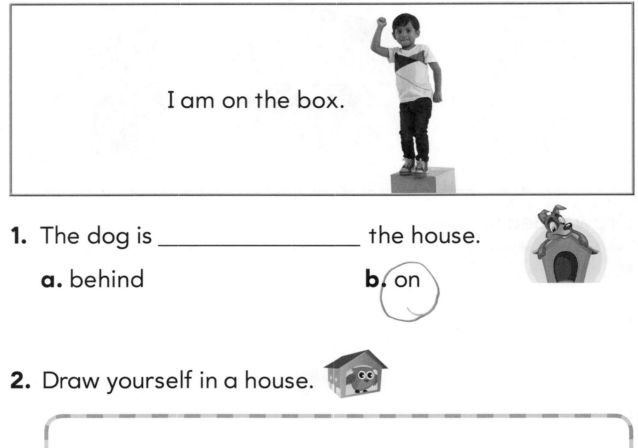

I am on the box.

1. The dog is _____ the house.

   a. behind   **b.** on

2. Draw yourself in a house.

51392—180 Days of Social Studies   © *Shell Education*

Name: _____ **Date:** _____

Directions: Look at the pictures. Match the pictures that are alike.

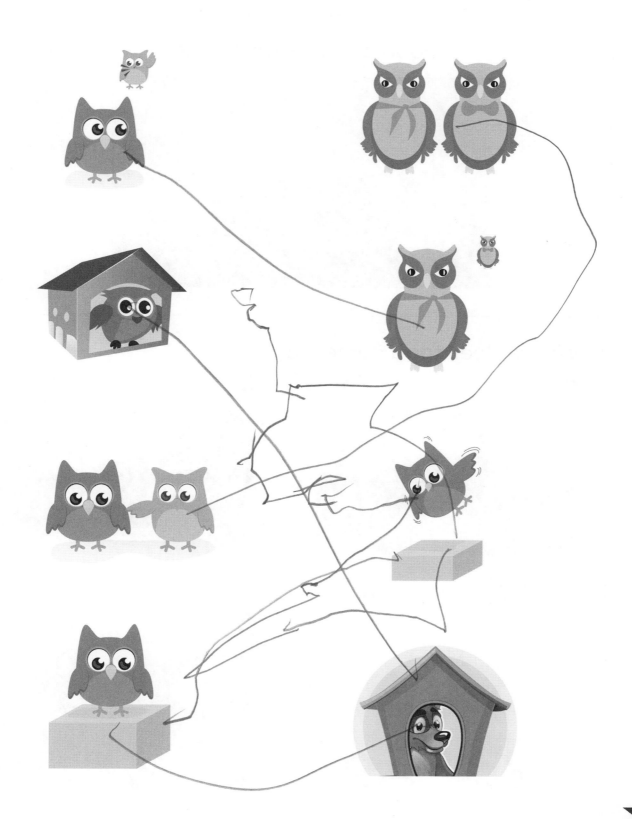

Economics

Name: _____ **Date:** _____

Directions: Look at the picture. Read the words. Circle the correct answers.

Food comes from farms.

1. Where does food come from?

   a.

   b.

   b.

2. What do farms grow?

   a.

   b.

Name: _____ **Date:** _____

Directions: Look at the pictures. Read the words. Circle the correct answers.

Economics

Food goes to stores.

1. Which comes first?

a.

 b.

2. Which comes next?

a.

b.

Economics

Name:_____ Date:_____

Directions: Look at the pictures. Read the words.
Circle the correct answer.

We buy food. We bring it home.

1. Where do we buy food?

a.

 b.

2. Draw the food you like to buy.

Name: _____ **Date:** _____

Directions: Look at the pictures. Read the words.

We cook.   We eat.

Draw foods you like to eat.

Draw foods you do not like to eat.

Economics

Name: _____ **Date:** _____

Directions: Look at the pictures. How do we get food? Match the pictures with the numbers from first to last. Then, color the pictures.

Name:_____ **Date:**_____

Directions: Look at the picture. Read the words. Circle the correct answers.

America Says Thank You

We have holidays to say thank you. We say thank you to helpers. We say thank you for food. We like to eat food.

1. Who do we thank?

    a. toys

    b. soldiers

2. Why do people say thank you for food?

    a. They are happy to have food.

    b. They want more candy.

Name: _____ **Date:** _____

Directions: Look at the picture. Read the words. Circle the correct answers.

The First Thanksgiving

People helped each other. They said thank you.
We say thank you on Thanksgiving Day.

1. Why did they say thank you?
   a. for food   **b.** for ships

2. What did they eat?
   a.   **b.**

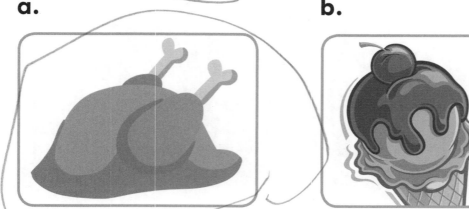

51392—180 Days of Social Studies

Name: _____ **Date:** _____

Directions: Look at the picture. Read the words. Circle the correct answer.

Memorial Day

We remember people who helped us. We say thank you.

1. What do we put on graves on Memorial Day?

   a. paint

   b. flags

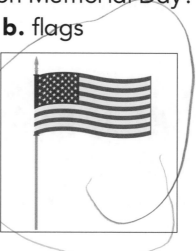

2. Draw yourself saying thank you.

History

Name: _____ **Date:** _____

Directions: Look at the picture. Read the words. Circle the correct answer.

This is Veterans Day. We say thank you. We honor people.

1. Circle the picture of veterans.

a.

b.

2. Draw a picture to give to a veteran.

51392—180 Days of Social Studies

© *Shell Education*

Name:_____ **Date:**_____

Directions: Circle people at school who you thank.

Civics

Name: _____ **Date:** _____

Directions: Look at the pictures. Read the words. Circle the correct answers.

Walking feet is a rule. Rules keep us safe.

1. Who is safe?

   a.

                               b.

2. Who is happy that he followed the rule?

   a.

                               b.

51392—180 Days of Social Studies

Name:_____ Date:_____

Directions: Look at the pictures. Read the words. Circle the correct answers.

Rules help our family.

1. Who is listening at home?

a.

b.

2. Who is happy?

a.

b.

Name:_____ **Date:**_____

Directions: Look at the pictures. Read the words. Circle the correct answer.

Rules help us have fun.

1. Who is sharing?

a.

b.

2. Draw yourself sharing at school.

Name:_____ **Date:**_____

Directions: Look at the pictures.

Civics

Rules

Draw one rule in your class.

© Shell Education

51392—180 Days of Social Studies

Civics

Name: _____ **Date:** _____

Directions: Circle the children following rules to stay safe.

Draw a picture of what the other child should do to be safe.

51392—180 Days of Social Studies

Name: _____ **Date:** _____

Directions: Look at the pictures. Read the words. Circle the correct answers.

my classroom

1. What do you see?

   a. chair   **b.** globe

2. What do you see?

   a. sign   **b.** drawers

Name:_____ **Date:**_____

Directions: Look at the pictures. Read the words. Circle the correct answers.

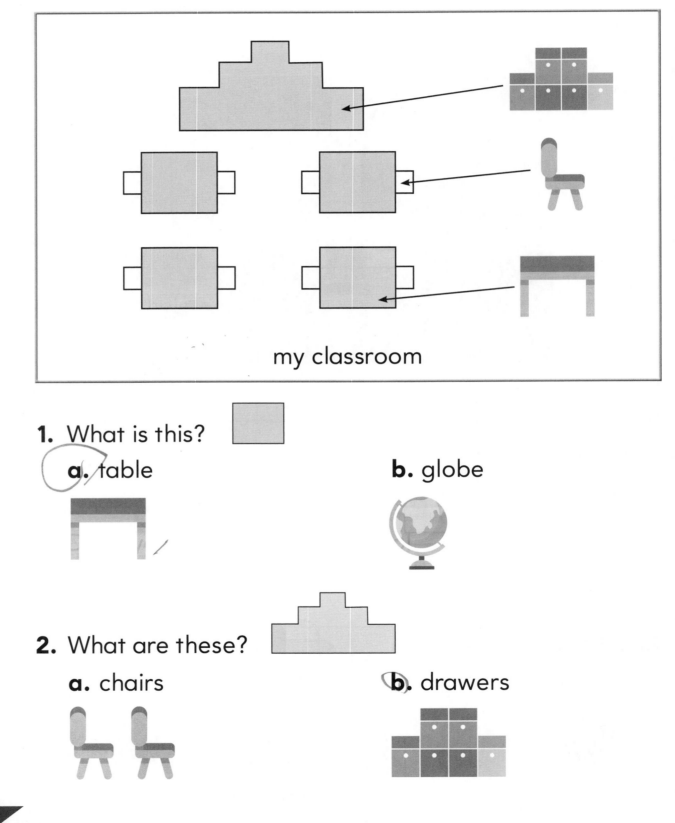

my classroom

1. What is this?

a. table

b. globe

2. What are these?

a. chairs

b. drawers

51392—180 Days of Social Studies

Name:_____ **Date:**_____

Directions: Look at the picture. Read the words.

Here is a classroom.

Draw a map of this classroom.

Name: _____ **Date:** _____

Geography

Directions: Look at the picture. Read the words.

Draw a map of your classroom.

Name:_____ **Date:**_____

Directions: Look at the pictures. Circle things you should put on a map of a classroom.

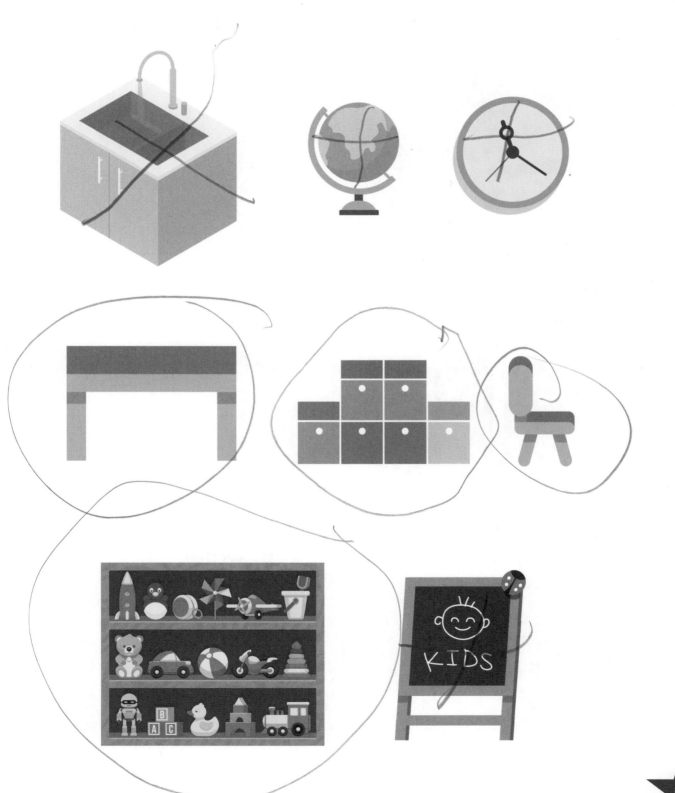

Economics

Name: _____ **Date:** _____

Directions: Look at the pictures. Read the words.
Circle the correct answers.

We need water.

I want these treats!

1. What do I need?

a. soda

b. water

2. What do I want?

a. ice cream cone

b. water

Name: _____ **Date:** _____

Directions: Look at the pictures. Read the words. Circle the correct answers.

I need food.   I want treats.

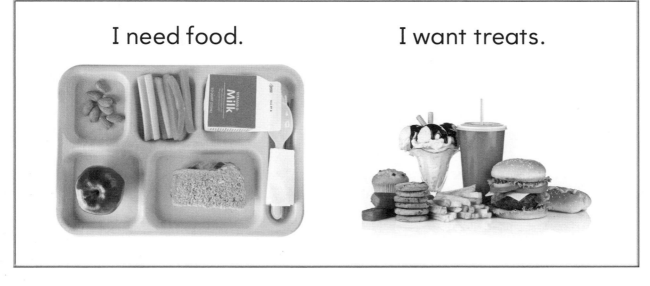

1. Which food is good for me?
   a. apple   **b.** ice cream

2. What do I want?
   a. water   **b.** cookie

Economics

Name:_____ **Date:**_____

Directions: Look at the pictures. Read the words. Circle the correct answer.

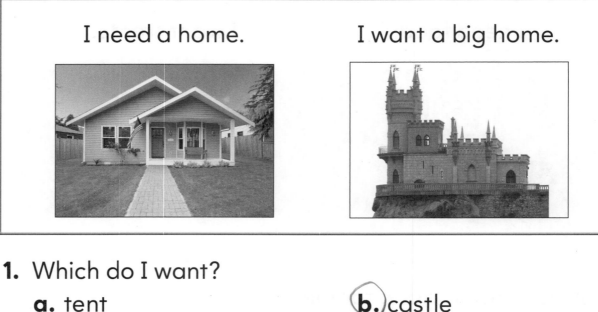

I need a home.

I want a big home.

1. Which do I want?

a. tent

b. castle

2. Draw the house you want.

51392—180 Days of Social Studies

© *Shell Education*

Name:_____ **Date:**_____

Directions: Look at the pictures. Read the words.

I need clothes for sun. I need clothes for rain.
I need clothes for cold.

Draw the clothes you need for a hot day.

Economics

Name: _____ **Date:** _____

Directions: Look at the pictures. Cut ✂--- out the pictures. Paste GLUE them in the correct boxes.

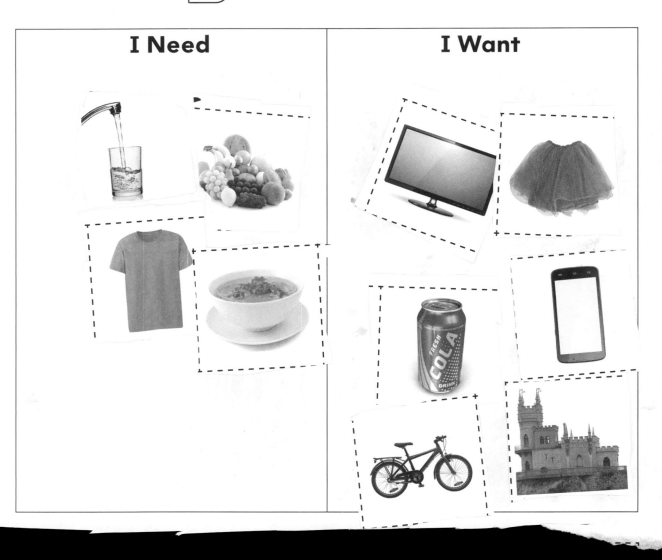

I Need	I Want

Name:_____ **Date:**_____

Directions: Read the words. Answer the questions.

We have symbols. We like our country.

1. Why do we have symbols?
   a. We like to talk.   **b.** We like our country.

2. Which is a symbol of our country?
   a.   **b.**

History

Name:_____ **Date:**_____

Directions: Look at the picture. Read the words. Circle the correct answers.

Our flag has red stripes. It has white stripes. The flag has 50 white stars.

1. Why is our flag called the Stars and Stripes?

   a. The flag is big and has three colors.

   b. The flag has 50 stars and 13 stripes.

2. Which sentence is true?

   a. The flag has 13 stripes.

   b. The flag has 100 white stars.

Name:_____ **Date:**_____

Directions: Look at the picture. Read the words. Circle the correct answer.

History

The bald eagle is a bird. It lives for a long time. The bald eagle is strong and free. It tells us that we are strong and free, too.

1. What is true?

   a. The bald eagle is free.

   b. The dog is free.

2. Draw a pet that could be a symbol of our country.

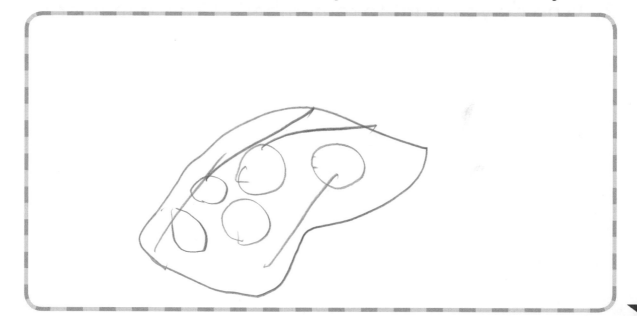

History

Name:_____ Date:_____

Directions: Look at the pictures. Answer the questions.

This is the Lincoln Memorial.

Lincoln's face is on the penny.

1. Who is on the penny?

a. George Washington

b. Abraham Lincoln

2. Who do you want to remember? Draw a memorial.

51392—180 Days of Social Studies   © Shell Education

Name: _____ **Date:** _____

Directions: Look at the picture. Read the words. Match the words with the right pictures.

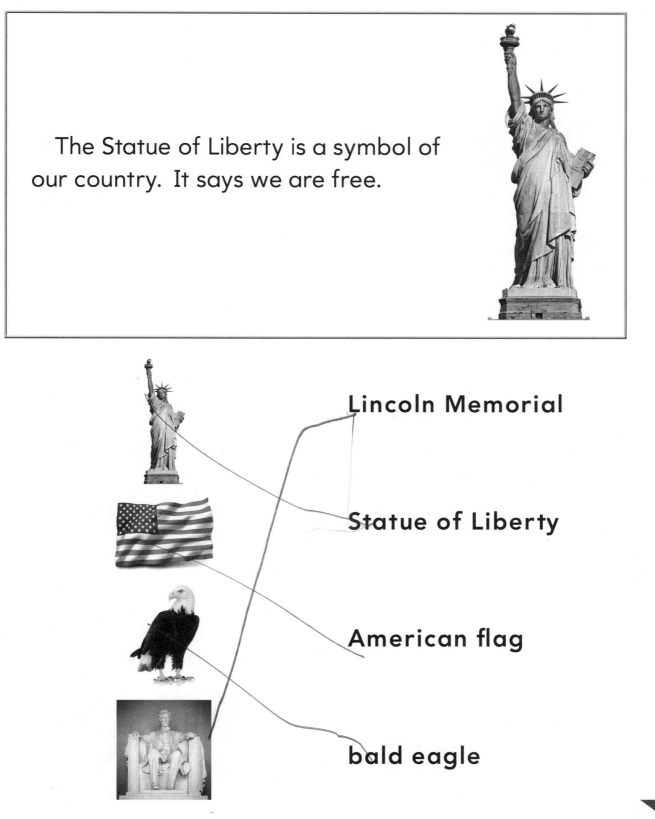

The Statue of Liberty is a symbol of our country. It says we are free.

Lincoln Memorial

Statue of Liberty

American flag

bald eagle

Civics

Name: _____ **Date:** _____

Directions: Look at the pictures. Read the words.
Answer the questions.

We are Americans. We try to be good citizens.
We try to help.

1. Who is helping?

a.

b.

2. Who are being good citizens?

a.

b.

Name:_____ **Date:**_____

Directions: Look at the pictures. Read the words.
Answer the questions.

We share.

1. Who is sharing?

a.

b.

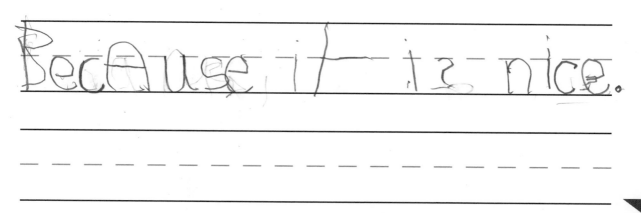

C

2. Why should we share?

BecAuse it is nice.

_____

_ _ _ _ _ _ _ _ _ _ _ _ _ _ _

_____

Civics

Name:_____ **Date:**_____

Directions: Look at the pictures. Read the words. Answer the question.

We help.

1. Who is helping?

a.

b.

2. Draw yourself helping at school.

51392—180 Days of Social Studies   © *Shell Education*

Name:_____ **Date:**_____

Directions: Look at the pictures. Read the words.

We get along.

Draw yourself playing with friends.

Name: _____ **Date:** _____

Civics

Directions: Look at the pictures. Circle the children who are being helpful citizens.

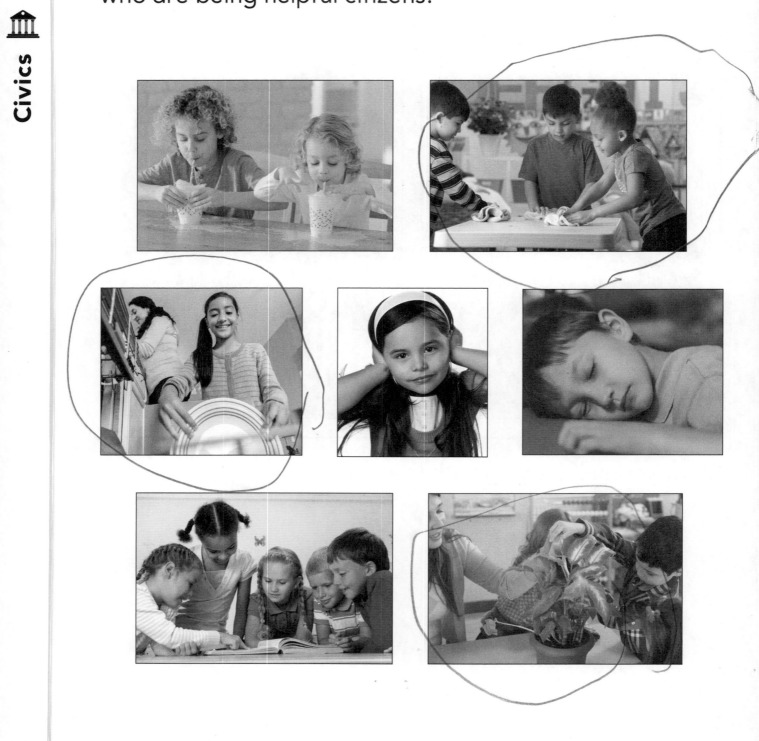

Name:_____ **Date:**_____

Directions: Look at the pictures. Read the words. Answer the questions.

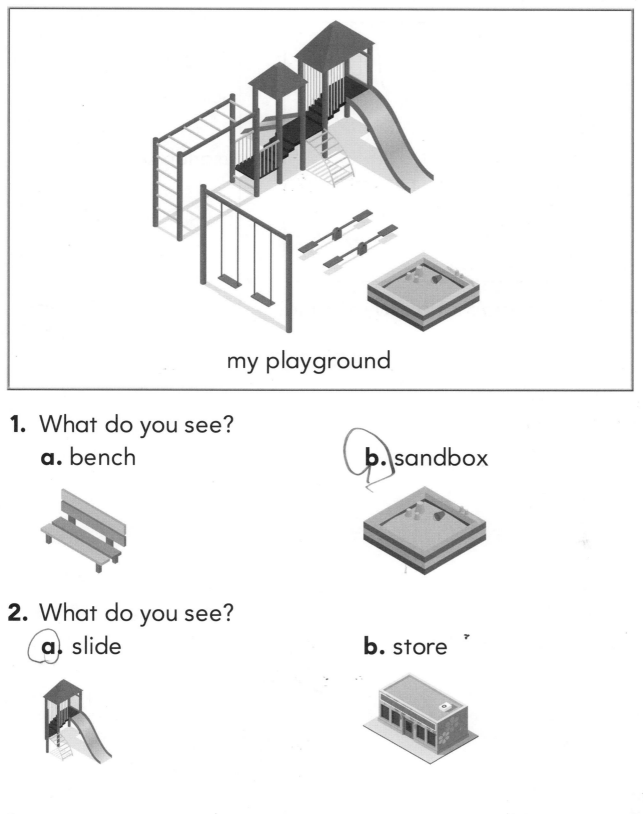

my playground

1. What do you see?
   a. bench

   b. sandbox

2. What do you see?
   a. slide

   b. store

Name: _____ **Date:** _____

Geography

Directions: Look at the pictures. Read the words. Answer the questions.

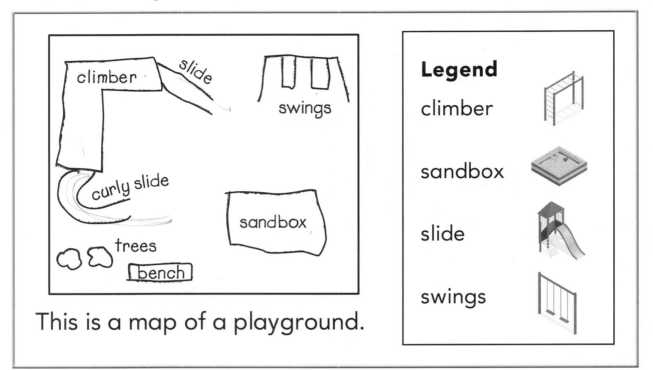

This is a map of a playground.

1. 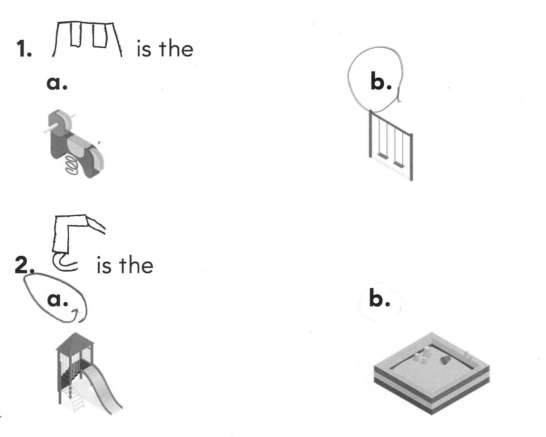 is the

   a.

   b.

2. is the

   a.

   b.

51392—180 Days of Social Studies

Name: _____ **Date:** _____

Directions: Look at the picture. Read the words.

Here is a playground.

1. Draw a map of this playground.

© Shell Education

51392—180 Days of Social Studies

Geography

Name:_____ **Date:**_____

Directions: Look at the picture. Read the words.

This is a map of my playground.

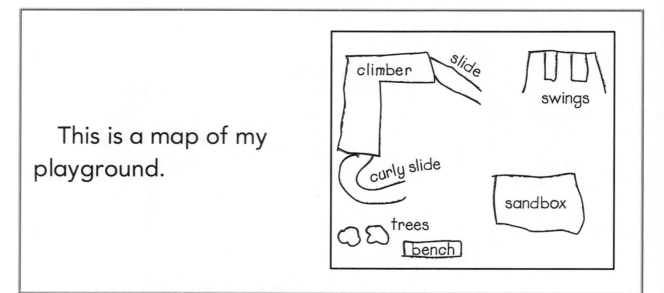

1. Draw a map of a playground you would like to play in.

51392—180 Days of Social Studies

© *Shell Education*

Name:_____ **Date:**_____

Directions: Look at the pictures. Circle things you could put on a map of a playground.

Name:_____ Date:_____

Directions: Look at the pictures. Read the words. Answer the questions.

They are helpers.

1. Who is the helper?
   a. jogger

   b. firefighter

2. Who needs the helper?
   a.

   b.

Name:_____ **Date:**_____

Directions: Look at the pictures. Read the words.
Answer the questions.

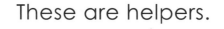

These are helpers.

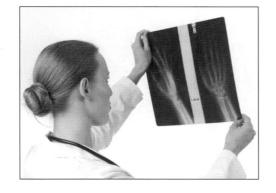 

1. Who is a helper?

a. doctor

b. swimmer

2. Who needs the helper?

a.

b.

Economics

Name: _____ **Date:** _____

Directions: Look at the pictures. Read the words. Answer the question.

They are helpers.

1. Who is the helper?

   a. sunbather

   b. police officer

2. Draw a police officer helping someone.

Name:_____ **Date:**_____

Directions: Look at the picture. Read the words.

This is a school helper.

1. Draw your teacher helping you at school.

Name: _____ **Date:** _____

Directions: Look at the pictures. Circle the helpers.

Economics

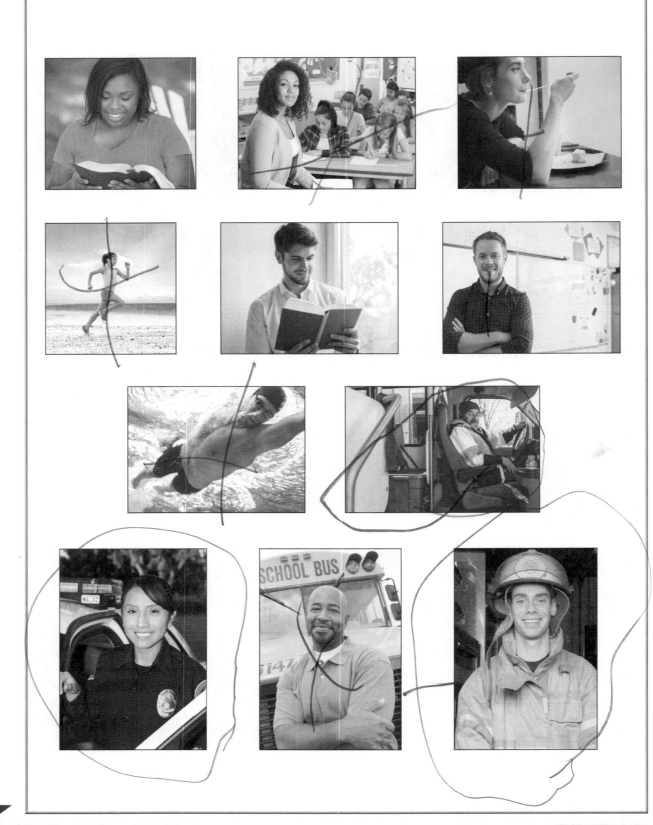

Name: _____ **Date:** _____

Directions: Look at the pictures. Read the words. Answer the questions.

We have symbols. We are proud of our country.

1. Why do we have symbols?
   a. We are proud of our country.

   b. We like to write.

2. Which is a symbol of our country?

   a.

   b.

© Shell Education

History

Name: _____ **Date:** _____

Directions: Look at the pictures. Read the words. Answer the questions.

America's Song
We have a song. The song is about our flag. We sing our song together. We are proud of our country.

---

1. What is our song about?

a. our school

b. our flag

2. Which is true?

a. We sing our song together.

b. Our song is funny.

Name: _____ **Date:** _____

Directions: Look at the pictures. Read the words. Answer the questions.

American flower

The rose is our flower. It means love. We are nice to each other We love our country.

1. Which is true?
   a. The rose means love.

   b. The rose means I am sad.

2. Draw a picture to show yourself being nice.

History

Name: _____ **Date:** _____

Directions: Look at the pictures. Read the words.

We have symbols. Our symbols show we are proud of our country.

1. Draw a symbol of our country. Label your picture.

Name: _____ **Date:** _____

Directions: Circle the pictures of our symbols.

Civics

Name: _____ **Date:** _____

Directions: Look at the pictures. Read the words. Answer the questions.

We help clean up.

1. Who is helping?

a.

b.

2. How do you help at home?

_____

_____

_____

_____

_____

Name:_____ **Date:**_____

Directions: Look at the pictures. Read the words. Answer the questions.

We recycle.

1. Who is recycling?

a.

b.

2. Where do we put an empty can?

a. recycling bin

b. paper bag

Civics

Name: _____ **Date:** _____

Directions: Look at the pictures. Read the words. Answer the question.

We help clean up.

1. Who is helping?

   a.

   b.

2. Draw yourself cleaning up.

51392—180 Days of Social Studies

© *Shell Education*

Name:_____ **Date:**_____

Directions: Look at the pictures. Read the words.

We look after our school.

1. How do you look after your school? Draw a picture.

Name:_____ **Date:**_____

Directions: Look at the pictures. Cut ✂---them out and paste [GLUE]▷ them where they go.

Name:_____ **Date:**_____

Directions: Look at the pictures. Read the words. Answer the questions.

land	water

1. Which picture shows land?
   a.   b.

2. Which picture shows water?
   a.   b.

51392—180 Days of Social Studies

Name:_____ Date:_____

Directions: Look at the pictures. Read the words. Answer the question.

Geography

Land

mountain   hill   volcano   plains

1. Which picture shows land?

   a.

   b.

2. Draw a volcano.

51392—180 Days of Social Studies

© *Shell Education*

Name:_____ **Date:**_____

Directions: Look at the pictures. Read the words. Answer the question.

Water

ocean   river   lake

1. Which picture shows water?

   a.   b.

2. Draw a river.

Name: _PIP_

Date: 2/21

Directions: Look at the pictures. Read the words.

I live on a hill. I see a lake.

Draw the land you want to live on.

Geography

Name: PIPSIS **Date:** _____

Directions: Look at the pictures. Circle the ones
with water.

Name: _____ **Date:** _____

Directions: Look at the pictures. Read the words. Answer the questions.

> They are helpers. They help animals.
>
>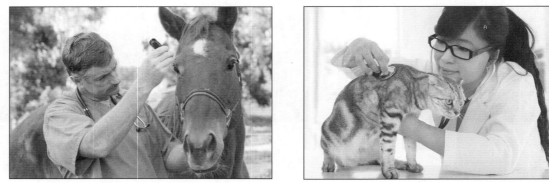

1. Who is the helper?

a.

b.

2. What needs the helper?

a.

b.

Name: _____ **Date:** _____

Directions: Look at the pictures. Read the words. Answer the questions.

> A dentist is a helper.
>
>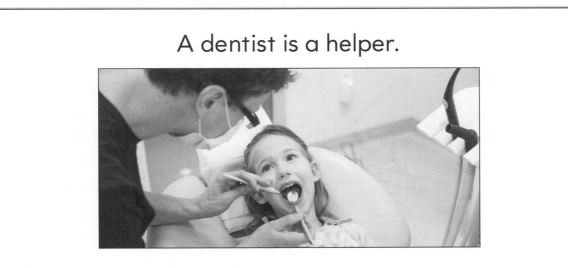

1. Who is the helper?

   a.

   b.

2. What does a dentist take care of?

   a.

   b.

   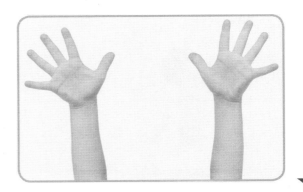

Economics

Name: _____ Date: _____

Directions: Look at the pictures. Read the words. Answer the questions.

They are helpers. They help clean up.

1. Who helps clean up?

a.

b.

2. Who is the helper?

a.

b.

Name:_____ **Date:**_____

Directions: Look at the picture. Read the words.

We help at school.

Draw yourself helping at school.

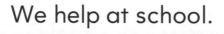

Name: _____ **Date:** _____

Directions: Look at the pictures. Match the helpers and their tools.

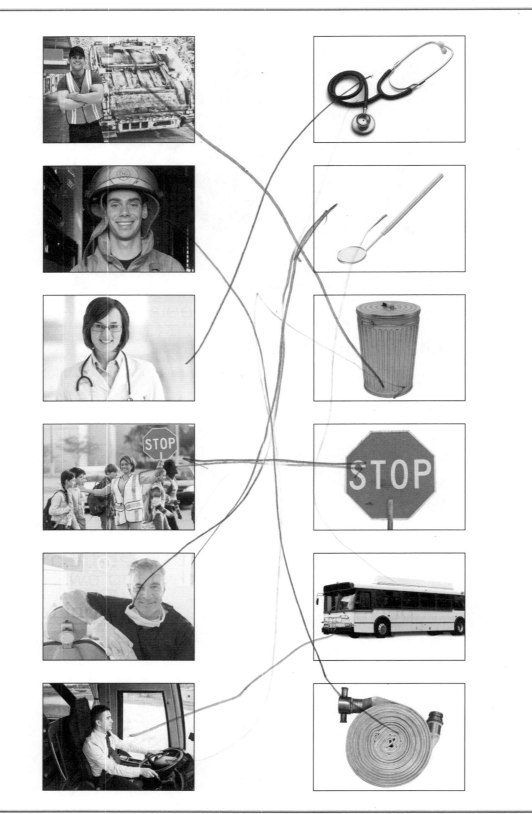

© Shell Education

Name: _____ **Date:** _____

Directions: Look at the pictures. Read the words. Answer the questions.

Thomas Edison
This is Thomas Edison.
He made the light bulb.

1. Match the pictures and people.

2. What can you make? Draw a picture.

History

Name: _____ **Date:** _____

Directions: Look at the pictures. Read the words. Answer the questions.

Henry Ford

This is Henry Ford.
He made the car.

1. What did Henry Ford make?

a. boat

b. car

2. What car do you like? Draw a picture of it.

Name: _____ **Date:** _____

Directions: Look at the pictures. Read the words.
Answer the questions.

We stand up tall. We pledge allegiance to the flag.

1. Circle people pledging allegiance to the flag.

a.

b.

2. Why do we say the pledge of allegiance?

_____

_ _

_____

_____

_ _

_____

Civics

Name:_____ **Date:**_____

Directions: Look at the picture. Read the words. Answer the question.

I say, "I love the flag."
I pledge allegiance to
our country. Look at
my hand.

1. Where is the boy's hand?
   a. on his heart   **b.** on his head

   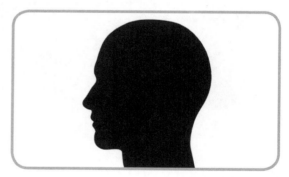

2. Draw a picture of yourself saying the pledge.

51392—180 Days of Social Studies   © *Shell Education*

Name: _____ **Date:** _____

Directions: Look at the picture. Read the words.

> We pledge allegiance to our flag and country. We live in one country together.
>
>

Draw a picture of one thing you love in our country.

Name:_____ Date:_____

Civics

Directions: Look at the pictures. Cut ✂---- out pledge pictures. Paste [GLUE]▷ them on this page.

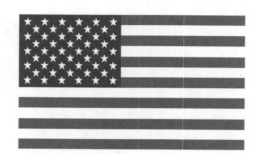

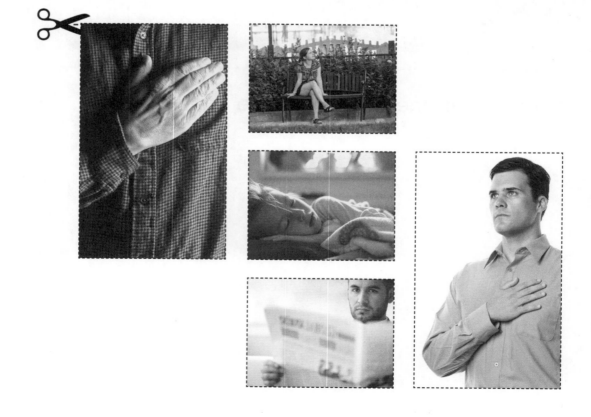

Name: _____ **Date:** _____

Directions: Look at the pictures. Read the words.
Answer the questions.

Geography

Land and Water

island   beach   canyon   waterfall

1. Which picture is a waterfall?

a.

b.

2. Which picture is a canyon?

a.

b.

Geography

Name: _____ **Date:** _____

Directions: Look at the pictures. Read the words. Circle and color the answers.

Here is a globe.   Here is a map.

1. Color the land on the globe.

2. Color the land on the map.

51392—180 Days of Social Studies

Name:_____ **Date:**_____

Directions: Look at the pictures. Read the words. Answer the questions.

Geography

High	Low

1. Which is high?

a.

b.

2. Write what low land looks like.

_____

- - - - - - - - - - - - - - - - - - -

_____

_____

- - - - - - - - - - - - - - - - - - -

_____

Geography

Name:_____ **Date:**_____

Directions: Look at the pictures. Read the words.

mountain   beach   canyon

Draw the land you want to visit. Name your picture.

51392—180 Days of Social Studies   © *Shell Education*

Name:_____ **Date:**_____

Directions: Look at the pictures. Cut 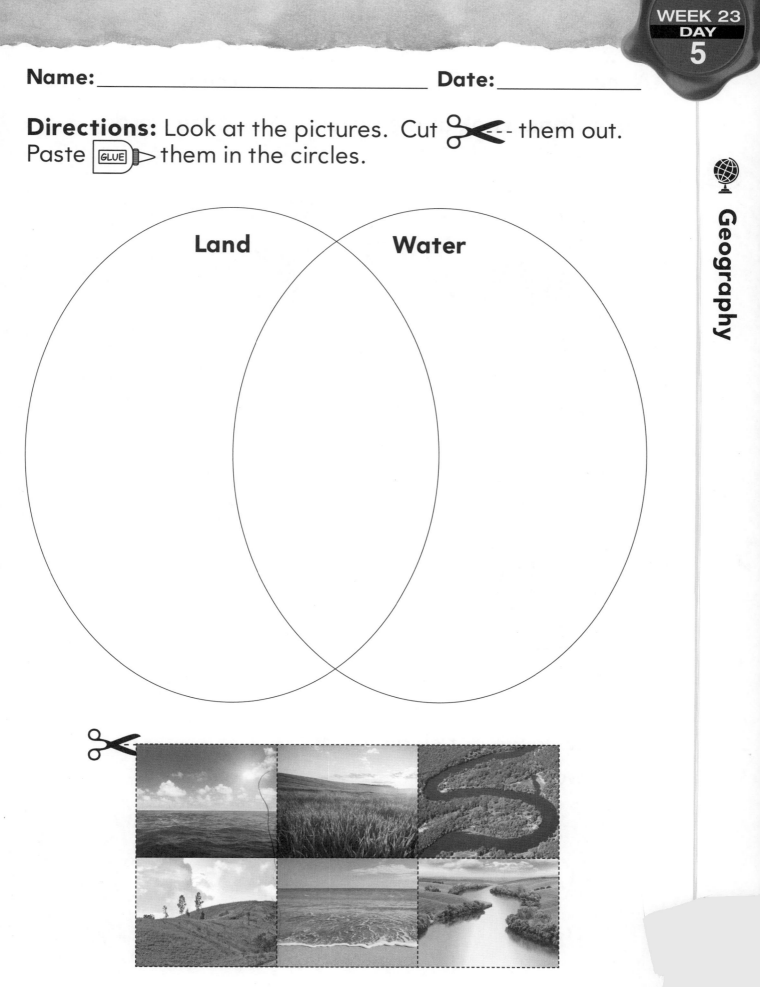--- them out. Paste them in the circles.

Land **Water**

Economics

Name: _____ **Date:** _____

Directions: Look at the pictures. Read the words. Answer the questions.

We need sleep.   We need clean hands.

1. How do we get sleep?

    a. in bed   **b.** jumping

2. How do we get clean hands?

    a. washing   **b.** playing

Name: _____ **Date:** _____

Directions: Look at the pictures. Read the words.
Answer the questions.

I am sick.

1. Which do I need?
   a. medicine

   b. sunglasses

2. Who can help me?
   a. jogger

   b. doctor

Economics

Name: _____ **Date:** _____

Directions: Look at the pictures. Read the words. Answer the question.

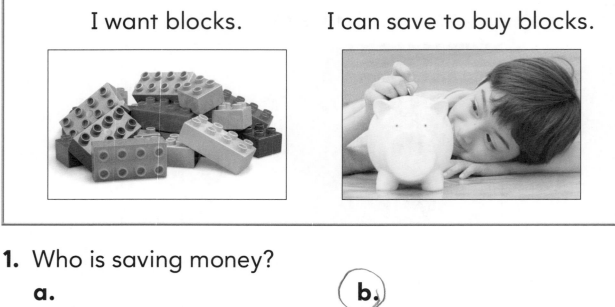

I want blocks.   I can save to buy blocks.

1. Who is saving money?

a.

b.

2. Draw a bank to save your money in.

Name: _____ **Date:** _____

Directions: Look at the pictures. Read the words.

I need a pencil at school. I want a blue pencil.

1. What does the boy want?

    a. a ball

   b. a blue pencil

2. What can the boy do to get the pencil he wants?

   _____

   _

   _____

   _

   _____

Economics

Name: _____ **Date:** _____

Directions: Look at the pictures. Match the needs and wants with solutions.

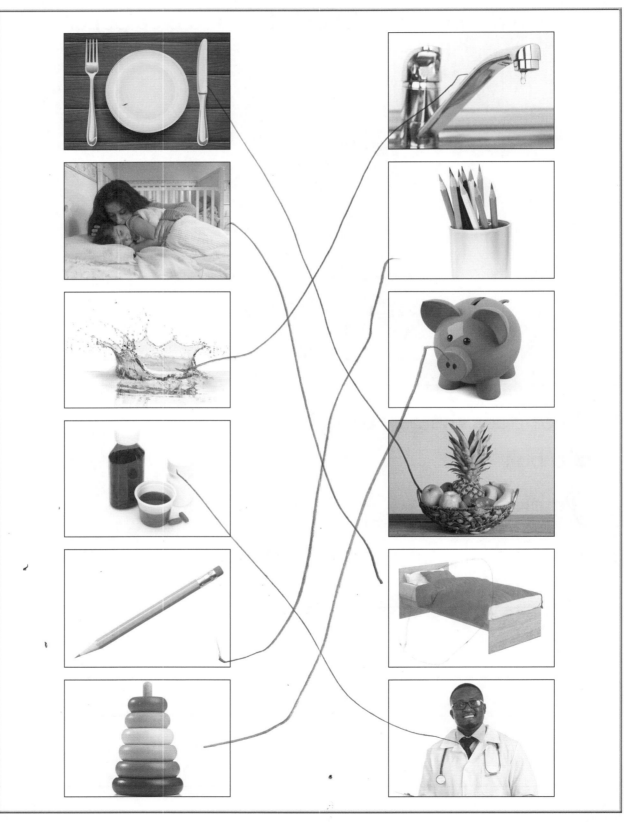

Name:_____ **Date:**_____

Directions: Look at the pictures. Read the words.
Answer the questions.

Going to Space

President Kennedy wanted Americans to go
to the moon. People made a rocket. They went to
the moon.

1. Where did the president want people to go?

a. to the moon

b. to the sun

2. What did they make?

a. a boat

b. a rocket

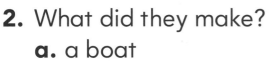

History

Name:_____ Date:_____

Directions: Look at the pictures. Read the words. Answer the questions.

Katherine Johnson

This is Katherine Johnson. She loves math. She helped the rockets go to the moon.

1. Which is a picture of Katherine Johnson?

a.

b.

2. What did Johnson do?

a. She helped rockets go to the moon.

b. She made candy.

Name:_____ **Date:**_____

Directions: Look at the picture. Read the words. Answer the question.

Neil Armstrong

This is Neil Armstrong. He went to the moon.

1. Where did Armstrong go?

a. to the sun

b. to the moon

2. Draw a rocket going to the moon.

History

Name: _____ **Date:** _____

Directions: Look at the pictures. Read the words. Answer the question.

Ellison Onizuka

This is Ellison Onizuka. He went to space.

1. Where did Onizuka go?

_____

— —

_____

2. Draw a picture of yourself in space.

Name: _____ **Date:** _____

Directions: Look at the pictures. Read the words.
Answer the questions.

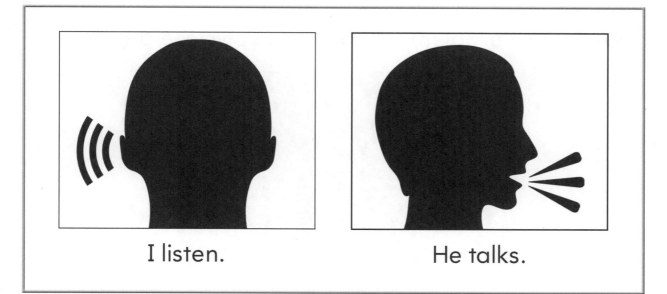

I listen.   He talks.

1. What can I do?

   a. not listen   **b.** listen

2. What can he do?

   a. not talk   **b.** talk

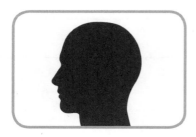
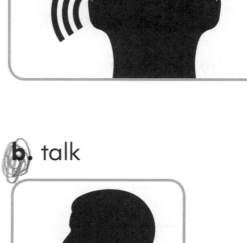

Civics

Name: _____ **Date:** _____

Directions: Look at the pictures. Read the words. Answer the questions.

We have a problem. We want to solve the problem.

1. What can the children do to solve their problem?
   a. argue with each other   **b.** take turns talking

 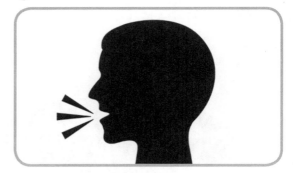

2. Why do they take turns listening?

   _____

   _

   _____

   _

   _____

51392—180 Days of Social Studies

© *Shell Education*

Name: _____ **Date:** _____

Directions: Look at the picture. Read the words. Answer the question.

I wait. We take turns.

1. Why do the girls wait and take turns?

_____

— — — — — — — — — — — — — — — —

_____

— — — — — — — — — — — — — — — —

_____

— — — — — — — — — — — — — — — —

_____

— — — — — — — — — — — — — — — —

_____

Civics

Name: _____ **Date:** _____

Directions: Look at the pictures. Cut ✂--- them out.
Paste [GLUE]▷ the steps in order.

| 1. | 2. |
| 3. | 4. |

Name:_____ **Date:**_____

Directions: Look at the pictures. Read the words. Answer the questions.

| winter | spring | summer | fall |

1. What do I wear in the winter?

a.

b.

2. What do I wear in the spring?

a.

b.

Geography

Name: _____ **Date:** _____

Directions: Look at the pictures. Read the words.
Answer the questions.

Cold Weather Clothes	Hot Weather Clothes

1. Which clothes are for cold weather?

   a. shorts   **b.** earmuffs

   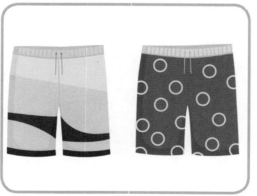   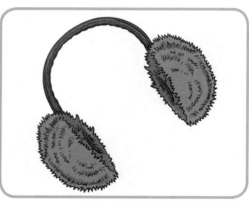

2. Which clothes are for hot weather?

   a. winter boots   **b.** bathing suits

   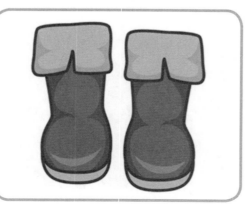   

Name:_____ **Date:**_____

Directions: Look at the pictures. Read the words. Answer the question.

Wet Weather Clothes

Dry Weather Clothes

Geography

1. Which is the rainy day?

a.

b.

2. Draw yourself in the rain.

Geography

Name:_____ **Date:**_____

Directions: Look at the pictures. Read the words.

We like summer weather.

We like winter weather.

Draw yourself in your favorite weather. Label your picture.

51392—180 Days of Social Studies

Name: _____ **Date:** _____

Directions: Look at the pictures. Cut ✂--- them out.
Paste GLUE⊳ them in the boxes.

winter	spring	summer	fall

Economics

Name: _____ **Date:** _____

Directions: Look at the pictures. Read the words.
Answer the questions.

We think about our choices.

1. Which is a good choice?
   a. potato chips   **b.** vegetables

2. Which is a bad choice?
   a. not sharing toys   **b.** sharing toys

Name:_____ **Date:**_____

Directions: Look at the pictures. Read the words.
Answer the questions.

We choose the things we want or need.

1. What could we choose at bedtime?

a. teddy bear

b. notebook and pencil

2. What could we choose at bath time?

a. towel

b. sun hat

Economics

Name:_____ **Date:**_____

Directions: Look at the pictures. Read the words.
Answer the question.

I want blueberries.

There are no blueberries in the store.

I can go to another store.

I can buy strawberries in the store I am in.

1. What would you do?
   a. Go to another store.
   b. Buy strawberries in the store you are in.

2. Draw your choice. Label it.

Name: _____ **Date:** _____

Directions: Look at the pictures. Read the words.

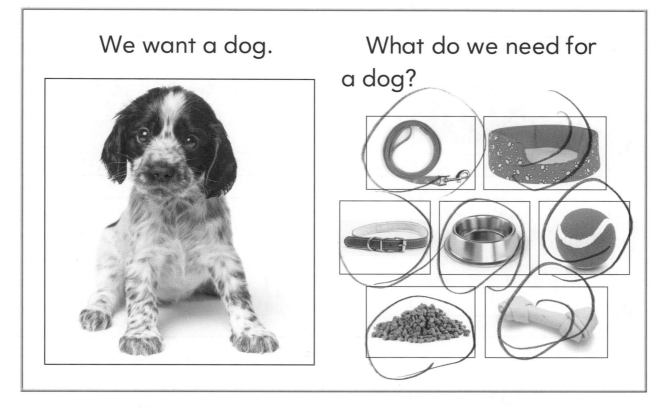

We want a dog.

What do we need for a dog?

Draw a dog and three things the dog needs.

Name:_____ Date:_____

Economics

Directions: Choose your favorite. Pick one on each row.

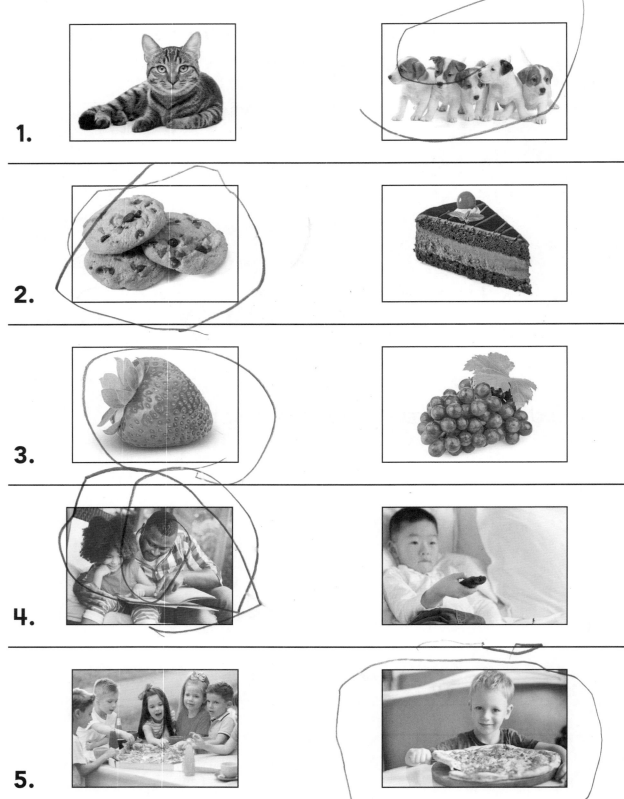

1.

2.

3.

4.

5.

Name: _____ **Date:** _____

Directions: Look at the pictures. Read the words.
Answer the questions.

Working Long Ago

Long ago, dads and moms worked. Children
worked, too. They helped gather crops and feed
animals.

1. Who worked long ago?
   a. baby   **b.** child

2. What did a child do long ago?
   a. rode a bike   **b.** fed chickens

51392—180 Days of Social Studies

History

Name: _____ **Date:** _____

Directions: Look at the pictures. Read the words. Answer the question.

Clothes Long Ago   **Clothes Today**

1. What did girls wear long ago?

a. bonnet   **b.** sun hat

2. Draw a hat that you like to wear.

Name:_____ **Date:**_____

Directions: Look at the picture. Read the words. Answer the questions.

Traveling Long Ago

1. How did people go places long ago?

a. by car

b. by horse and wagon

2. How do you go places? Draw a picture.

History

Name: _____ **Date:** _____

Directions: Look at the pictures. Read the words. Answer the question.

Going to School Long Ago

Children went to school long ago. They had a teacher. They learned many things.

1. Where did children go long ago?

a. to school

b. to the mall

2. Draw your classroom.

Name: _____ **Date:** _____

Directions: Cut out ✂---- the pictures. Paste [GLUE]> them in the boxes.

Long Ago	Today

History

Civics

Name: Pip   **Date:** _____

Directions: Look at the pictures. Read the words. Answer the questions.

It is circle time in our class. We can read a book. We can sing a song.

1. What time is it for the class in the story?

a. recess   **b.** circle time

2. What can we do at circle time?

a. Listen to a story.   **b.** Eat lunch.

160

Name: PIP   **Date:** 5/10

Civics

Directions: Look at the picture. Read the words. Answer the questions.

Seven children want to read. Two want to sing. We will read the book.

1. Which is more?

a.

2

b.

7

2. What will our class do?

READ

Civics

Name:_____ **Date:**_____

Directions: Look at the picture. Read the words. Answer the questions.

Our class voted for our snack today.

Snack Today

Suri
Tasha
Sam
Ethan
Lucas
Emily
Carlos
Marcus
Juan

1. Which snack would you vote for?

a. apple

b. banana

2. What will we have for a snack? Tell why.

_____

_ _

_____

_ _

_____

Name:_____ **Date:**_____

Directions: Look at the pictures. Read the words.

I want to ride my bike.

Anne wants to go to the park.

Anne is my friend. What should we do?
Draw and label a picture.

Civics

Name: _____ **Date:** _____

Directions: Look at the pictures. Read the words. Write the words **first**, **second**, or **third** beside the pictures.

We vote.

_____

- - - - - - - - - - - - -

_____

We think about our choices.

_____

- - - - - - - - - - - - -

_____

We play at recess.

_____

- - - - - - - - - - - - -

_____

51392—180 Days of Social Studies

Name: _____ **Date:** _____

Directions: Look at the pictures. Answer the question.

Building My School

1. What did they build?

a.

b.

2. Label the pictures.

_____

- - - - - - - - - - -

_____

_____

- - - - - - - - - - -

_____

Word Bank

forest   road

Geography

Name:_____ **Date:**_____

Directions: Look at the pictures. Read the words. Answer the question.

We built a garden.

1. What did we have first?

a.

b.

2. Label the pictures.

_____

- - - - - - - - - - - -

_____

_____

- - - - - - - - - - - -

_____

Word Bank

garden   field

Name:_____ **Date:**_____

Directions: Look at the pictures. Read the words.

We make trash.   We recycle trash.

Draw yourself recycling.

Geography

Name:_____ **Date:**_____

Directions: Look at the pictures. Read the words. Draw yourself taking care of the environment.

We plant trees.   We recycle.

Draw yourself taking care of the environment. Label your picture.

Name: _____ **Date:** _____

Directions: Look at the pictures. Circle the pictures of people helping the environment.

Geography

Economics

Name:_____ **Date:**_____

Directions: Look at the pictures. Read the words. Answer the questions.

I see a duck. I want the duck.

"I want money" says the man.

1. Which do I want?

a. robot

b. duck

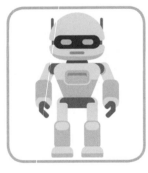

2. Why does the man say, "I want money"?

_____

_ _ _ _ _ _ _ _ _ _ _ _ _ _ _ _ _ _ _ _

_____

Name:_____ **Date:**_____

Directions: Look at the pictures. Read the words. Answer the questions.

I want the duck.

"It is $1.00" says the man.

1. What does the man want?

a. money

b. book

2. What do I need to buy the duck?

_____

_ _ _ _ _ _ _ _ _ _ _ _ _ _ _ _ _ _ _

_____

Economics

Name: _____ **Date:** _____

Directions: Look at the pictures. Read the words. Answer the questions.

The man wants money.	I save money.

1. Who wants the money?

a. man

b. police officer

2. How can I save money?

_____

_____

_____

_____

_____

Name: _____ **Date:** _____

Directions: Look at the pictures. Read the words.

I want the duck.　　　I save money.　　　I get the duck.

Draw what you would buy. Label the picture.

Economics

Name:_____ Date:_____

Directions: Look at the pictures. Cut ✂--- them out.
Paste GLUE▷ them in order.

1	2
3	4

51392—180 Days of Social Studies   © *Shell Education*

Name: _____ **Date:** _____

Directions: Look at the pictures. Read the words.
Answer the questions.

Bringing the Mail

long ago   today

1. How did people bring mail long ago?

a. by horse   **b.** by car

2. Draw how you get mail.

History

Name: _____ **Date:** _____

Directions: Look at the pictures. Read the words. Answer the question.

long ago today

Teachers

1. Which is a teacher from the past?

a.

b.

2. Draw your teacher.

Name: _____ **Date:** _____

Directions: Match the pictures of jobs.

Jobs Long Ago and Jobs Today

Civics

Name: _____ **Date:** _____

Directions: Look at the pictures. Read the words. Answer the question.

We respect the flag.

We respect our country.

We take care of our country.

U.S.A.

1. How do we take care of our country?

_____

- - - - - - - - - - - - - - - - - - - -

_____

_____

- - - - - - - - - - - - - - - - - - - -

_____

Name: _____ **Date:** _____

Directions: Look at the pictures. Read the words. Answer the questions.

We show respect.
We listen.

We say we are sorry.

1. How do we show respect for each other?

a. We comb our hair.

b. We listen.

2. What do we say if we have not been respectful?

_____

_ _ _ _ _ _ _ _ _ _ _ _

_____

Civics

Name: _____ **Date:** _____

Directions: Look at the pictures. Read the words. Answer the questions.

We show respect. We help.

1. How is she showing respect for her home?

_____

- - - - - - - - - - - - - - - - - - - -

_____

- - - - - - - - - - - - - - - - - - - -

_____

2. How is he showing respect at home?

_____

- - - - - - - - - - - - - - - - - - - -

_____

- - - - - - - - - - - - - - - - - - - -

_____

51392—180 Days of Social Studies

Name: _____ **Date:** _____

Directions: Look at the picture. Read the words.

We show respect. I help. I play with the baby.

Draw what you do at home to show respect.

Civics

Name:_____ **Date:**_____

Directions: Look at the pictures. Circle the ways we can show respect.

1. How do you show respect?

_____

_ _

_____

Name: _____ **Date:** _____

Directions: Look at the pictures. Read the words.
Answer the questions.

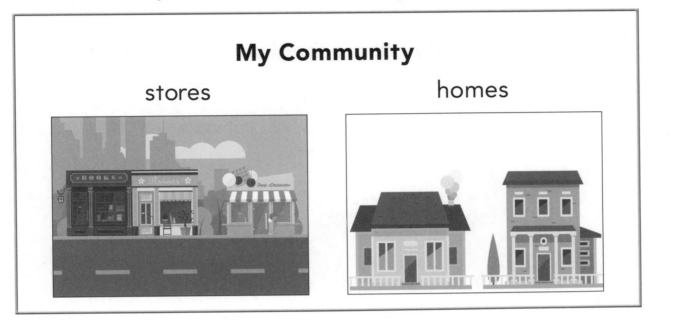

My Community

stores   homes

1. What are two places in your community?

_____

- -

_____

- -

_____

2. Where do you go in your community?

_____

- -

_____

Geography

Name: _____ **Date:** _____

Directions: Look at the pictures. Read the words. Answer the questions.

My community has a school and a fire station.

1. Where does the teacher work?

a. ice cream shop   **b.** school

2. Where do they keep fire trucks?

_____

_ _

_____

Name: _____ **Date:** _____

Directions: Look at the pictures. Read the words.
Answer the questions.

People go to
the park. There
are lots of things
to do there.

1. Write two things you can see people doing in this
park.

_____

_ _

_____

_ _

_____

2. Circle things in the picture you can do at a park.

Geography

Name:_____ **Date:**_____

Directions: Look at the pictures. Read the words.

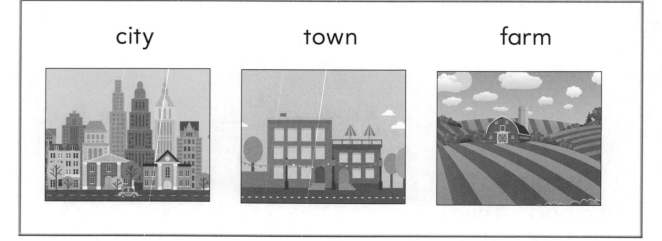

city   town   farm

Draw where you live. Write about where you live.

_____

- -

_____

- -

_____

51392—180 Days of Social Studies

Name:_____ **Date:**_____

Directions: Look at the pictures. Circle things in your community. Write about one of the pictures you circled.

_____

- -

_____

- -

_____

- -

_____

- -

_____

Name: _____ **Date:** _____

Economics

Directions: Look at the pictures. Read the words.
Answer the questions.

Our country has money.
We have coins.

Some coins are small.   Some coins are big.

penny   dime   quarter   nickel

1. Which coin is small?
   a. quarter   **b.** dime

2. What is the name of a big coin?

_____

_____

_____

51392—180 Days of Social Studies

Name:_____ **Date:**_____

Directions: Look at the pictures. Read the words.
Answer the questions.

We have pennies.
Pennies are small.

We have nickels.
Nickles are big.

1. A penny is

a. big   **b.** small

2. Which coin would you like? Why?

_____

- -

_____

_____

- -

_____

- -

_____

Economics

Name: _____ **Date:** _____

Directions: Look at the pictures. Read the words. Answer the questions.

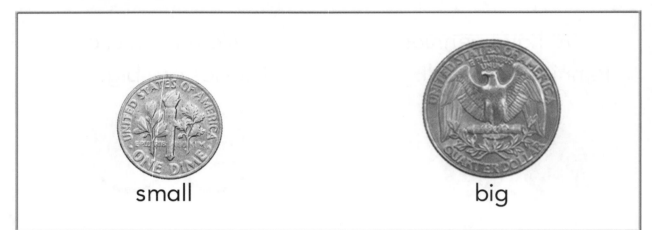

small   big

1. Which coin is small?

   a.   **b.**

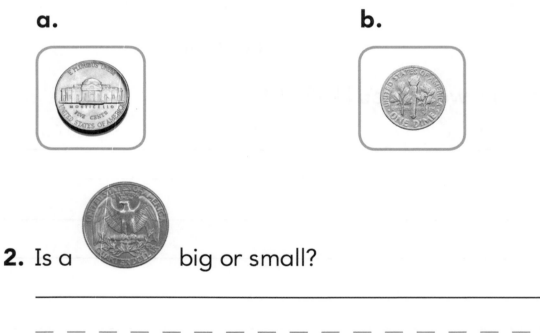

2. Is a   big or small?

_____

_ _

_____

51392—180 Days of Social Studies

Name: _____ **Date:** _____

Directions: Look at the pictures. Cut ✂ --- them out. Paste [GLUE]▷ them in the correct boxes.

small coins	big coins

✂

1. What is your favorite coin?

_____

_ _

_____

Name:_____ **Date:**_____

Directions: Look at the pictures. Match the coins to the words.

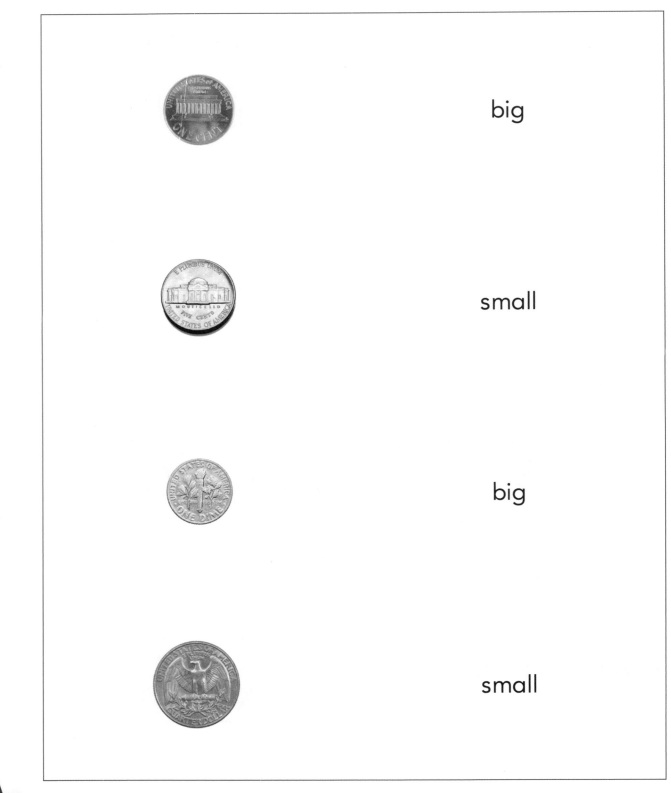

big

small

big

small

ANSWER KEY

Week 1—History

Day 1
Baby 1
Adult woman 2
Elderly man 3

Day 2
1. a
2. b

Day 3
1. b
2. Drawings will vary.

Day 4
First: baby
Now: child
Next: teen

Day 5
Drawings will vary.

Week 2—Civics

Day 1
1. a
2. a; allow for b

Day 2
1. a
2. a

Day 3
1. b
2. Drawings will vary.

Day 4
Drawings will vary.

Day 5
Drawings will vary.

Week 3—Geography

Day 1
1. a
2. b

Day 2
1. b
2. a

Day 3
1. owl in front of block; dog in front of house
2. Drawings of bear under table will vary.

Day 4
1. b
2. Drawings will vary.

Day 5
Matching: 1 and 3; 2 and 4; 3 and 1; 4 and 2

Week 4—Economics

Day 1
1. a
2. b

Day 2
1. b
2. b

Day 3
1. b
2. Drawings will vary.

Day 4
Drawings will vary.

Day 5
Circled: plate of food, carrots, shoes, houses, water, fruit, pants

ANSWER KEY *(cont.)*

Week 5—History

Day 1
1. a
2. a

Day 2
1. a
2. b

Day 3
1. a
2. a

Day 4
1. a
2. Drawings will vary.

Day 5
Drawings will vary.

Week 6—Civics

Day 1
1. a
2. b

Day 2
1. a
2. b

Day 3
1. b
2. Drawings will vary.

Day 4
Drawings will vary.

Day 5
Circled: boy and girl
Drawings will vary.

Week 7—Geography

Day 1
1. b
2. b

Day 2
1. a
2. a

Day 3
1. owl on box; dog on house
2. Drawings will vary.

Day 4
1. b
2. Drawings will vary.

Day 5
Matching: 1 and 2; 2 and 4; 3 and 1; 4 and 3

Week 8—Economics

Day 1
1. a
2. b

Day 2
1. b
2. b

Day 3
1. b
2. Drawings will vary.

Day 4
Drawings will vary.

Day 5
farm: 1
grocery store: 2
eating at the table: 3

ANSWER KEY *(cont.)*

Week 9—History

Day 1
1. b
2. a

Day 2
1. a
2. a

Day 3
1. b
2. Drawings will vary.

Day 4
1. b
2. Drawings will vary.

Day 5
Circle: custodian; crossing guard; bus driver

Week 10—Civics

Day 1
1. b
2. a

Day 2
1. b
2. a

Day 3
1. b
2. Drawings will vary.

Day 4
Drawings will vary.

Day 5
Circle 2nd and 3rd images.
Drawings will vary.

Week 11—Geography

Day 1
1. a
2. b

Day 2
1. a
2. b

Day 3
Maps will vary.

Day 4
Maps will vary.

Day 5
Responses will vary; allow for circling all the images.

Week 12—Economics

Day 1
1. b
2. a (allow for b)

Day 2
1. a
2. b (allow for a)

Day 3
1. b (allow for a)
2. Drawings will vary.

Day 4
Drawings will vary.

Day 5
Needs: fruit; shirt; soup; tutu
Wants: soda; TV; bicycle; cell phone

ANSWER KEY *(cont.)*

Week 13—History

Day 1
1. b
2. a

Day 2
1. b
2. a

Day 3
1. a
2. Drawings will vary.

Day 4
1. b
2. Drawings will vary.

Day 5
Matching: 1 and 2; 2 and 3; 3 and 4; 4 and 1

Week 14—Civics

Day 1
1. a
2. b

Day 2
1. a
2. Responses will vary.

Day 3
1. b
2. Drawings will vary.

Day 4
Drawings will vary.

Day 5
Circle: loading dishwasher; sitting and listening; sharing

Week 15—Geography

Day 1
1. b
2. a

Day 2
1. a
2. a

Day 3
Maps will vary.

Day 4
Maps will vary.

Day 5
Circle: picnic table; sandbox; swing set; climber; trees; merry-go-round; seesaw; allow for store

Week 16—Economics

Day 1
1. b
2. a

Day 2
1. a
2. a

Day 3
1. b
2. Drawings will vary.

Day 4
Drawings will vary.

Day 5
Circle: teachers; police officer; bus driver; fire fighter

ANSWER KEY *(cont.)*

Week 17—History

Day 1
1. a
2. a

Day 2
1. b
2. a

Day 3
1. a
2. Drawings will vary.

Day 4
Drawings and labels will vary.

Day 5
Circle: Statue of Liberty; bald eagle;
Lincoln Memorial; flag; girl with flag;
Washington Memorial

Week 18—Civics

Day 1
1. b
2. Responses will vary.

Day 2
1. b
2. a

Day 3
1. b
2. Drawings will vary.

Day 4
Drawings will vary.

Day 5
Recycling box: paper, soda can
Trash can: banana peel
Shelf: blocks, toy car

Week 19—Geography

Day 1
1. b
2. b

Day 2
1. b
2. Drawings will vary.

Day 3
1. b
2. Drawings will vary.

Day 4
Drawings will vary.

Day 5
Circle all land images; allow for images that
show water and land.

Week 20—Economics

Day 1
1. a
2. b

Day 2
1. b
2. a

Day 3
1. b
2. b

Day 4
Drawings will vary.

Day 5
Matching: 1 and 3; 2 and 6; 3 and 1; 4 and 4;
5 and 2; 6 and 5

ANSWER KEY *(cont.)*

Week 21—History

Day 1
1. b
2. Responses will vary.

Day 2
1. b
2. a

Day 3
1. light bulb and Edison; flag and Betsy Ross
2. Drawings will vary.

Day 4
1. b
2. Drawings will vary.

Day 5
Students should circle the flag, old car, and lightbulb. Drawings will vary.

Week 22—Civics

Day 1
1. a
2. b

Day 2
1. b
2. Responses will vary.

Day 3
1. a
2. Drawings will vary.

Day 4
Drawings will vary.

Day 5
Pasted pictures associated with the pledge of allegiance

Week 23—Geography

Day 1
1. a
2. a

Day 2
1. Landmasses circled
2. Water around the continents colored

Day 3
1. a
2. Responses will vary.

Day 4
Drawings and labels will vary.

Day 5
Left circle: all land images; right circle: all water images; center: images that include both land and water

Week 24—Economics

Day 1
1. a
2. a

Day 2
1. a
2. b

Day 3
1. b
2. Drawings will vary.

Day 4
1. a
2. Responses will vary.

Day 5
Matching: 1 and 4; 2 and 5; 3 and 1; 4 and 6; 5 and 2; 6 and 3

ANSWER KEY *(cont.)*

Week 25—History

Day 1
1. a
2. b

Day 2
1. a
2. a

Day 3
1. b
2. Drawings will vary.

Day 4
1. to space
2. Drawings will vary.

Day 5
Matching:1 and My name is _____; 2 and
Ellison Onizuka; 3 and Neil Armstrong;
4 and President Kennedy; 5 and
Katherine Johnson

Week 26—Civics

Day 1
1. b
2. b

Day 2
1. b
2. b

Day 3
1. b
2. Responses will vary.

Day 4
Responses will vary.

Day 5
1. They argue; 2. One talks; 3. One listens;
4. They play together.

Week 27—Geography

Day 1
1. a
2. b

Day 2
1. b
2. b

Day 3
1. a
2. Drawings will vary.

Day 4
Drawings will vary.

Day 5
Drawings will vary.

Week 28—Economics

Day 1
1. b
2. a

Day 2
1. a
2. a

Day 3
1. Allow for a or b.
2. Drawings and labels will vary.

Day 4
Drawings will vary.

Day 5
Responses will vary.

ANSWER KEY *(cont.)*

Week 29—History

Day 1
1. b
2. b

Day 2
1. a
2. Drawings will vary.

Day 3
1. b
2. Drawings will vary.

Day 4
1. a
2. Drawings will vary.

Day 5
Long ago: log cabin; wagon; child in field
Today: students with computers; bicycle rider; students in classroom

Week 30—Civics

Day 1
1. b
2. a

Day 2
1. b
2. Responses will vary.

Day 3
1. Allow for a or b.
2. Student should note that more students voted for banana.

Day 4
Drawings and labels will vary. Students may note that they could ride to the park.

Day 5
Vote: second; thinking about choices: first; playing at recess: third

Week 31—Geography

Day 1
1. a
2. b

Day 2
1. b
2. b

Day 3
Drawings will vary.

Day 4
Drawings and labels will vary.

Day 5
Circle gardening and recycling pictures.

Week 32—Economics

Day 1
1. b
2. Responses may vary. Students should note that the man wants money.

Day 2
1. a
2. money

Day 3
1. a
2. Responses will vary.

Day 4
Drawings and labels will vary.

Day 5
1. wants duck; 2. saves; 3. gives money;
4. is happy

ANSWER KEY *(cont.)*

Week 33—History

Day 1
1. a
2. answers will vary

Day 2
1. a
2. Drawings and labels will vary.

Day 3
1. a
2. Drawings and responses will vary.

Day 4
1. a
2. Drawings will vary.

Day 5
Matching: 1 and 4; 2 and 5; 3 and 1; 4 and 3;
5 and 2

Week 34—Civics

Day 1
1. recycle; pick up garbage

Day 2
1. b
2. "Sorry"; allow for other responses

Day 3
1. Responses will vary; cleaning up
2. Responses will vary; washing dishes

Day 4
Drawings will vary.

Day 5
Circle: pledging allegiance; cleaning up;
helping with sibling; recycling
1. Responses will vary.

Week 35—Geography

Day 1
1. Responses will vary.
2. Responses will vary.

Day 2
1. b
2. fire station or fire hall

Day 3
1. Responses will vary.
2 Responses will vary.

Day 4
Drawings and responses will vary.

Day 5
Responses will vary.

Week 36—Economics

Day 1
1. b
2. quarter or nickel

Day 2
1. b
2. Responses will vary.

Day 3
1. b
2. big

Day 4
Small coins: dimes; pennies
Big coins: nickels; quarters
1. Responses will vary.

Day 5
Matching: penny and dime to small; nickel and
quarter to big.

Response Rubric

Teacher Directions: The answer key provides answers for the multiple-choice and short-answer questions. This rubric can be used for any open-ended questions where student responses vary. Evaluate student work to determine how many points out of 12 students earn.

Student Name: _____

	4 Points	3 Points	2 Points	1 Point
Content Knowledge	Gives right answers. Answers are based on text and prior knowledge.	Gives right answers based on text.	Gives mostly right answers based on text.	Gives incorrect answers.
Analysis	Thinks about the content, and draws strong inferences/ conclusions.	Thinks about the content, and draws mostly correct inferences/ conclusions.	Thinks about the content, and draws somewhat correct inferences/ conclusions.	Thinks about the content, and draws incorrect inferences/ conclusions.
Explanation	Explains and supports answers fully.	Explains and supports answers with some evidence.	Explains and supports answers with little evidence.	Provides no support for answers.

Total: _____

Practice Page Item Analysis

Teacher Directions: Record how many multiple-choice questions students answered correctly. Then, record their rubric totals for Day 5. Total the four weeks of scores, and record that number in the Overall column.

Circle Week Range: 1–4 5–8 9–12 13–16 17–20 21–24 25–28 29–32 33–36						
Student Name	**Day 1** Text Analysis	**Day 2** Text Analysis	**Day 3** Primary Source or Visual Text	**Day 4** Making Connections	**Day 5** Synthesis and Application	**Overall**
Ryan	1, 2, 2, 3	2, 2, 2, 2	2, 2, 1, 2	1, 1, 2, 1	12, 10, 12, 12	73

Student Item Analysis By Discipline

Teacher Directions: Record how many multiple-choice questions students answered correctly. Then, record their rubric totals for Day 5. Total the four weeks of scores, and record that number in the Overall column.

Student Name:

History Weeks	Day 1 Text Analysis	Day 2 Text Analysis	Day 3 Primary Source or Visual Text	Day 4 Making Connections	Day 5 Synthesis and Application	Overall
1						
5						
9						
13						
17						
21						
25						
29						
33						

Civics Weeks	Day 1 Text Analysis	Day 2 Text Analysis	Day 3 Primary Source or Visual Text	Day 4 Making Connections	Day 5 Synthesis and Application	Overall
2						
6						
10						
14						
18						
22						
26						
30						
34						

Student Item Analysis By Discipline *(cont.)*

Student Name:						
Geography Weeks	**Day 1** Text Analysis	**Day 2** Text Analysis	**Day 3** Primary Source or Visual Text	**Day 4** Making Connections	**Day 5** Synthesis and Application	**Overall**
3						
7						
11						
15						
19						
23						
27						
31						
35						
Economics Weeks	**Day 1** Text Analysis	**Day 2** Text Analysis	**Day 3** Primary Source or Visual Text	**Day 4** Making Connections	**Day 5** Synthesis and Application	**Overall**
4						
8						
12						
16						
20						
24						
28						
32						
36						

Digital Resources

To access the digital resources, go to this website and enter the following code: 96136590 .
www.teachercreatedmaterials.com/administrators/download-files/

Rubric and Analysis Sheets

Resource	Filename
Response Rubric	responserubric.pdf
Practice Page Item Analysis	itemanalysis.pdf
	itemanalysis.docx
	itemanalysis.xlsx
Student Item Analysis by Discipline	socialstudiesanalysis.pdf
	socialstudiesanalysis.docx
	socialstudiesanalysis.xlsx

Standards and Themes

Resource	Filename
Weekly Topics and Themes	topicsthemes.pdf
Standards Charts	standards.pdf